A2

English Literature
for AQA A

Tony Childs
Jackie Moore

Heinemann

Heinemann Educational Publishers
Halley Court, Jordan Hill, Oxford OX2 8EJ
A division of Reed Educational and Professional Publishing Ltd

OXFORD MELBOURNE AUCKLAND
JOHANNESBURG BLANTYRE GABORONE
IBADAN PORTSMOUTH (NH) USA CHICAGO

First published 2001

05 04 03 02 01
10 9 8 7 6 5 4 3 2 1

ISBN 0 435 132288

Acknowledgements

The publishers gratefully acknowledge the following for permission to reproduce copyright material. Every effort has been made to trace copyright holders, but in some cases has proved impossible. The publishers would be happy to hear from any copyright holder that has not been acknowledged.

Extract from *Translations* by Brian Friel, published by Faber and Faber Ltd. Reprinted with permission of the publisher. Extract from 'Twelve Songs IX' by W. H. Auden, published by Faber and Faber Ltd. Reprinted by permission of the publisher. 'Valentine' by Carol Ann Duffy, from *Mean Time* by Carol Ann Duffy, published by Anvil Press Poetry Ltd in 1993. Reprinted by permission of Anvil Press Poetry Ltd. Extract from *Birdsong* by Sebastian Faulks, published by Hutchinson. Used by permission of The Random House Group Ltd. Extract from *Sons and Lovers* by D. H. Lawrence, published by Cambridge University Press. Reprinted by permission of Laurence Pollinger Ltd and the Estate of Frieda Lawrence Ravagli. Extract from *To The Lighthouse* by Virginia Woolf. Reprinted by permission of The Society of Authors as the Literary Representative of the Estate of Virginia Woolf. Extract from *A Suitable Boy* by Vikram Seth. Reprinted by permission of The Orion Publishing Group Ltd. Extract from *The Color Purple* by Alice Walker, published by The Women's Press. Reprinted by permission of David Higham Associates Ltd. Extract from *Oranges Are Not the Only Fruit* by Jeannette Winterson, published by Vintage. Reprinted by permission of Margaret Reynolds. Extract from *An Inspector Calls* by J. B. Priestley, copyright © J. B. Priestley 1947. Reproduced by permission of Peters Fraser & Dunlop on behalf of the Estate of J. B. Priestley. Extract from *Sacred Hunger* by Barry Unsworth, published by Penguin Books. Copyright © Barry Unsworth. Reprinted by permission of Penguin Books Ltd. Extract from *Hawksmoor* by Peter Ackroyd, published by Random House. Copyright © Peter Ackroyd. Reprinted by permission of Sheil Land Associates Ltd. Extract from *Nineteen Eighty-Four* by George Orwell, copyright © George Orwell 1949. By permission of Bill Hamilton as the Literary Executor of the Estate of the late Sonia Brownell Orwell and Martin Secker & Warburg Ltd c/o A. M. Heath & Co. Ltd. Extracts from *Brave New World* by Aldous Huxley. Reprinted by permission of The Reece Halsey Agency, Los Angeles. Extract from *The Great Gatsby* by F. Scott Fitzgerald, published by Heinemann. Reprinted by permission of David Higham Associates Ltd. Extract from *Death of a Salesman* by Arthur Miller. Copyright © 1949 by Arthur Miller. Reproduced by permission of the author c/o Rogers, Coleridge & White Ltd, 20 Powis Mews, London W11 1JN. In association with International Creative Management, New York. Extract from *Captain Corelli's Mandolin* by Louis de Bernières, published by Vintage (May 1995). Used by permission of The Random House Group Ltd. Extract from *Catch-22* by Joseph Heller. Copyright © Joseph Heller 1955. Reprinted by permission of A. M. Heath & Co. Ltd. Extracts from various Siegfried Sassoon poems: 'Lamentations', 'Attack', 'Suicide in the Trenches', 'Base Details' and 'A Footnote to War'. Copyright Siegfried Sassoon, by kind permission of George Sassoon, c/o Barbara Levy Literary Agency, London. Extract from *Journey's End* by R. C. Sherriff. Copyright © R. C. Sherriff 1929. Reproduced with permission of Curtis Brown Group Ltd, London on behalf of the Estate of R. C. Sherriff. Extract from *Oh, What a Lovely War!* by Joan Littlewood, published by Methuen. Reprinted by permission of the publishers. Extract from *The Accrington Pals* by Peter Whelan, published by Methuen. Reprinted by permission of the publishers. Extract from *Letters from a lost generation: the First World War letters of Vera Brittain and four friends* edited by Bishop and Bostridge. Reprinted with the kind permission of Mark Bostridge. Extract from 'Afterwards' by Margaret Cole, published by Allen & Unwin in *Poems*. Reprinted by permission of David Higham Associates Ltd. Extracts from *Goodbye to all that* by Robert Graves, published by Carcanet Press Ltd. Reprinted by permission of the publishers. Extract from *Tommy Goes to War* by M. Brown, published by J. M. Dent. Reprinted by permission of The Orion Publishing Group Ltd. 'The Silent One' by Ivor Gurney, from *The Great War in British Literature*, published by Cambridge University Press. Extract from *The Ghost Road* by Pat Barker, published by Viking. © Pat Barker. Reprinted by permission of Penguin Books Ltd. 'Winter warfare' by Edgell Rickword, from *Collected Poems*, published by Carcanet Press Ltd. Reprinted by permission of the publishers. Extract from *Not About Heroes* by Stephen MacDonald, published by Faber and Faber Ltd. Reprinted by permission of the publishers. *Isabella and the Pot of Basil* by William Holman Hunt, Laing Art Gallery, Tyne and Wear Museums

Typeset by TechType, Abingdon, Oxon
Printed and bound in the United Kingdom by Bath Press

Contents

How this book will help you in your course

This book is designed to help students following AQA Specification A in Advanced English Literature through their course. Most students approaching this specification will already have studied AQA Specification A in AS English Literature, and so this book has been written with that in mind. It is important to recognise from the start, however, that A2 Level is different from AS Level, in that two of the Assessment Objectives change (see 'The key to success: the Assessment Objectives' on the next page). Remember too, that this book is not simply a guide to individual set texts – each of you will choose different texts to work on. Rather, it is a guide to what you have to do with your texts in order to succeed.

The rest of this introduction will deal with the Assessment Objectives for the specification. Don't overlook this introduction and go straight to the modules – the Assessment Objectives not only underpin all the work in the course, but an understanding of them is also the key to gaining good marks, as the marking is based entirely on them. The final module, Reading for Meaning, tests all the Objectives.

The main part of the book deals with each of the three assessment modules for the A2 course. For each module, the book will take you through its design and content, with practical advice and activities. The work you are asked to do will be tailored to the type of assessment involved in the module, which might be external assessment, either open or closed book, or coursework. There will also be examples of the sort of questions and tasks which will be used to test each module as part of the examination.

There is a Glossary on pages 195–196.

The key to success: the Assessment Objectives

Here are the Assessment Objectives for Advanced (A2) English Literature:

The examination will assess a candidate's ability to:
AO1   communicate clearly the knowledge, understanding and insight appropriate to literary study, using appropriate terminology and accurate and coherent written expression
AO2ii respond with knowledge and understanding to literary texts of different types and periods, exploring and commenting on relationships and comparisons between literary texts
AO3   show detailed understanding of the ways in which writers' choices of form, structure and language shape meanings
AO4   articulate independent opinions and judgements, informed by different interpretations of literary texts by other readers
AO5ii evaluate the significance of cultural, historical and other contextual influences on literary texts and study

What the new Assessment Objectives mean

The Assessment Objectives were dealt with in the book accompanying the AS specification, and you will have worked with them during your AS course. It is important to recognise, though, that at Advanced (A2) Level Assessment Objectives 2 and 5 change, and make new demands on students. At AS Level, Assessment Objective 2i asks candidates to '**respond with knowledge and understanding to literary texts of different types and periods**'. At A2 Level, '**exploring and commenting on relationships and comparisons between literary texts**' is added. As you can see, this is quite different, reintroducing the requirement to compare texts which you were probably used to in your GCSE English Literature course.

Assessment Objective 5i at AS Level asks candidates to '**show understanding of the contexts in which literary texts are written and understood**'. At A2 Level this becomes: '**evaluate the significance of cultural, historical and other contextual influences on literary texts and study**'. What you have to think about, therefore, is how various factors have shaped the writing of the texts you're studying – and how they affect your reading of them.

Here are some of the relevant types of context which you might look at:

- The context of a period or era, including significant social, historical, political and cultural processes, which might encompass period-specific styles. This might concern the period in which the work was written, or the period which is being written about. These may not be the same. A knowledge of the context of the slave trade, for instance, will certainly affect your reading of Barry Unsworth's *Sacred Hunger*, even though it was written in 1992.

- The context of the work in terms of the writer's biography or **milieu**. This might include literary and generic factors – how a play could be seen as a revenge tragedy, for instance, though this is also partly a period-specific context.

- The language context, including relevant episodes in the development and use of literary language, or the question of colloquial and **dialect** styles.

- The different contexts for a work established by its reception over time – works may have different meanings and effects upon their audience in different periods.

Just recognising the contexts of a text is not enough, though, because you have to 'evaluate the significance' of them. You need to decide how much a knowledge of the contexts affects the ways in which you understand the texts. Is a particular context of marginal significance, or is it central to your reading of the text?

Breaking down the Assessment Objectives

As you can see, the Assessment Objectives define the literary skills which you have to show during the course. It is vital to understand that the Assessment Objectives have different numbers of marks in different modules, and even for different texts. For example, in Module 4, Texts in Time, the 30 marks available are divided like this:

AO1   6 marks

AO2ii   5 marks

AO3   6 marks

AO4   7 marks

AO5ii   6 marks

This looks as though the marks are equally divided for each question, but this isn't quite the case. In this module, you have to choose a pre-1770 drama text and a pre-1900 poetry text. You'll be assessed on Assessment Objectives 1, 2ii and 3 on both texts – but on the drama text, you will also be assessed on AO4, making it the dominant Assessment Objective. For the poetry, AO4 (interpretations) isn't tested, but AO5ii (contexts) is.

So, the marks depend on the Assessment Objectives, and the marks vary between modules, and sometimes between sections too. That's why there is a box at the beginning of each of the three modules to show you exactly which Assessment Objectives count in that module, and how many marks each one carries.

An exercise in the new Advanced Level Assessment Objectives

STOP ALL THE CLOCKS, CUT OFF THE TELEPHONE

Stop all the clocks, cut off the telephone,
Prevent the dog from barking with a juicy bone,
Silence the pianos and with muffled drum
Bring out the coffin, let the mourners come.

Let aeroplanes circle moaning overhead
Scribbling on the sky the message He Is Dead,
Put crêpe bows round the white necks of the public doves,
Let the traffic policemen wear black cotton gloves.

He was my North, my South, my East and West,
My working week and my Sunday rest,
My noon, my midnight, my talk, my song;
I thought that love would last for ever: I was wrong.

The stars are not wanted now: put out every one;
Pack up the moon and dismantle the sun;
Pour away the ocean and sweep up the wood.
For nothing now can ever come to any good.

W. H. Auden (1907–73)

VALENTINE

Not a red rose or a satin heart.

I give you an onion.
It is a moon wrapped in brown paper.
It promises light
like the careful undressing of love.

Here.
It will blind you with tears
like a lover.
It will make your reflection
a wobbling photo of grief.

I am trying to be truthful.

Not a cute card or a kissogram.

I give you an onion.
Its fierce kiss will stay on your lips,
possessive and faithful
as we are,
for as long as we are.

Take it.
Its platinum loops shrink to a wedding-ring,
if you like.
Lethal.
Its scent will cling to your fingers,
cling to your knife.

Carol Ann Duffy (1955–   )

SONNET 18

Shall I compare thee to a summer's day?
Thou art more lovely and more temperate.
Rough winds do shake the darling buds of May,
And summer's lease hath all too short a date:
Sometime too hot the eye of heaven shines,
And often is his gold complexion dimm'd;
And every fair from fair sometime declines,
By chance, or nature's changing course, un-trimm'd;
But thy eternal summer shall not fade
Nor lose possession of that fair thou ow'st;
Nor shall Death brag thou wand'rest in his shade,
When in eternal lines to time thou grow'st;
 So long as men can breathe, or eyes can see,
 So long lives this, and this gives life to thee.

William Shakespeare (1564–1616)

Although you might have come across these poems before, the aim here is to look at them in the context of the Advanced (A2) Level Assessment Objectives.

AO2ii respond with knowledge and understanding to literary texts of different types and periods, exploring and commenting on relationships and comparisons between literary texts

The first step in comparing these poems is easy – all three are concerned with love and time. In addition, all three are personal, first-person poems: 'Stop All the Clocks' mourns the death of a loved one, and the other two make declarations of love, though not in a straightforward way. 'Valentine', particularly, concerns itself with the realities of love ('I am trying to be truthful'), meaning its difficulties and dangers.

To compare the poems in a detailed way, it's a good idea to use AO3 as a framework, comparing how the three poets use form, structure and language to shape their meanings. Work your way through the poems using the following suggestions.

Form

There are three different forms here – but remember, what you're interested in is comparing how form expresses meaning in each case.

1   The four separate verses of 'Stop All the Clocks' suggest each verse contains a separate aspect of the subject. Is this true here? How do punctuation and rhyme give a sense of finality?

2   'Sonnet 18' is unpunctuated by verse divisions. Is it one continuous argument? If it changes, is it marked by the form? How? Think about rhyme as well as the layout of the lines.

3   'Valentine' does not follow a set pattern of verse, or of rhyme, though there are repetitions and echoes. Can you find any of these? How does Carol Ann Duffy use the form to suggest unconnected but related thoughts about love, and about this relationship?

Now look back at your conclusions, and think about the relationships and comparisons between these texts.

Structure

Form is closely related to structure in all these poems.

4   You've already worked out the subjects of each of the verses in 'Stop All the Clocks'. Is there a logical structure here? How does the poem build to the last verse, and the last line in particular?

5   How does the first line of 'Sonnet 18' set the agenda for the whole poem? Where does the view of time alter, and which word at the beginning of a line marks the shift? The final change is to introduce the idea of the life of the poem, not just the person. Where does this begin, exactly?

6   'Valentine' looks different from the others on the page, not only because of the lack of verse pattern, but because of the varying line length. Look at the effects of some of the very short lines, and the three single lines. Why do you think the poem begins the way it does, and ends the way it does?

Now look back at your conclusions, and think about the relationships and comparisons between these texts.

Language

There's a lot to say about the ways in which language is used to express meaning in all of these poems. Here are a few questions to get you started.

7 Look at sentence forms in all three poems. Where can you find commands, or questions? Why have the poets used these forms?

8 Two of these poems make use of repetition, and one doesn't. What are the effects of the repetitions where they are used, and what does the lack of repetition tell you about the other one?

9 Each of the three poems has particular uses of language features. Look at the verbs in 'Stop All the Clocks', the unorthodox sentences in 'Valentine', and the word play in 'Sonnet 18'.

10 Imagery is a central feature of all three poems.

- Look at the imagery in the last two verses of 'Stop All the Clocks'. What is the effect of all of the images taken together? How does each one contribute to the whole? Notice particularly the line about the moon and the sun, bearing in mind the other two poems you're working on.

- The other two poems both take a single image and examine it. In 'Valentine', what gifts does the speaker reject? Why, do you think? Why does she find an onion appropriate, and what view of love does this reveal? Look at the further comparisons which stem from this central idea.

- 'Sonnet 18' also works on one image, introduced in the first line. As in 'Valentine', the conventional love comparison is rejected. Look at the ways in which Shakespeare uses the idea to praise the object of the poem, developing more imagery along the way.

Now look back at your conclusions, and think about the relationships and comparisons between these texts.

AO5ii	evaluate the significance of cultural, historical and other contextual influences on literary texts and study

At Advanced (A2) Level it is not enough simply to recognise the contexts of each text studied. You also have to evaluate their significance for your reading of the text, particularly as you start to think about forming an interpretation. The ideas and questions which follow should help you to see what this might mean, and to see how the Assessment Objectives are interrelated.

'Stop All the Clocks' is an interesting poem to start with, when thinking about contexts. You might already have two contexts for your reading of the text: as part of GCSE English Literature study, in which case you probably studied it in the context of other poems, or its reading in the film *Four Weddings and a Funeral*. If you've seen and heard it in the film, the context may well be significant in your response to it. In the film, the reading at the funeral is an emotional moment, designed to affect the audience, who may well also associate it with homosexual love. However, these first two verses of the poem were originally published, in the prose/verse drama *The Ascent of F6*, by W. H. Auden and Christopher Isherwood. If you read the rest of the poem in this original version, you might arrive at a different interpretation of the verses.

ACTIVITY

1 Re-read the first two verses of 'Stop All the Clocks' above, then read the following three verses, which completed the piece in *The Ascent of F6*.

> Hold up your umbrellas to keep off the rain
> From Doctor Williams while he opens a vein;
> Life, he pronounces, it is finally extinct.
> Sergeant, arrest that man who said he winked!
>
> Shawcross will say a few words sad and kind
> To the weeping crowds about the Master-Mind,
> While Lamp with a powerful microscope
> Searches their faces for a sign of hope.
>
> And Gunn, of course, will drive the motor-hearse:
> None could drive it better, most would drive it worse.
> He'll open up the throttle to its fullest power
> And drive him to the grave at ninety miles an hour.

2 The poem may well seem more like a satirical parody of love poetry now. How has the writer worked to create this tone? Think about:

- the effects of particular words
- the effects of particular rhymes
- the actions of the characters, and how they are described.

Clearly these two contexts give rise to interpretations which are quite opposed to each other. But this doesn't necessarily mean that the satirical reading of the poem is the 'right' one. If it did, it would mean that anybody's response to the poem based on the film alone would somehow be invalid. Assessment Objective 5i, the building block for this Objective, concerns 'the contexts in which literary texts are written and understood' – but these need not be the same. Here, the poem is written in one context, and understood in another by the film's audience. Two meanings – or interpretations – are generated, and both are valid. Nor does it make any difference that the writer did not intend, or indeed know about, the film context. Once a text is written, the writer is merely one interpreter of its meaning.

In the other two poems, gender provides an interesting context. Unlike 'Stop All the Clocks', neither poem identifies the gender of the person addressed. Some research could reveal significant contexts here. If you assume that the speaker in the poem – the persona – is the poet speaking (which might not be the case), what might the sexual preferences of the writers tell you? When you've looked at this, you might think about these issues:

1 Does this information make any difference to your reading of the poems? In other words, are the contexts significant?

2 If you respond to the poems differently when you know about these contexts, why do you respond differently? Is it to do with the poems, or with you?

3 What evidence are you using in reaching your conclusions about the poems? Context is a form of evidence in itself, as are the details of form, language and structure. The tone of 'Stop All the Clocks' can perhaps be read either way, depending on how you view the evidence. But what evidence of context can you find in the other two poems?

You could, of course, investigate other contexts, and if you were studying these texts as part of your Advanced (A2) Level course you would have to choose which to pursue – which contexts might prove to be significant in the writing and understanding of the texts. You could look at the features of each of the poems which place them in their historic and social contexts, for example. With the Shakespeare sonnet, you could look at the literary context of the sonnet form in Shakespeare's period, and how he uses it, or at how ambiguity appears in other Shakespeare sonnets. If you were tackling this as an Advanced (A2) Level task, you would also need to evaluate the significance of these contexts. Which are most central to your understanding of the texts, and why?

You will have noticed that as you investigated and thought about contexts, more relationships and comparisons between the three texts occurred to you, taking you back to AO2ii. The Advanced (A2) Level course, like the AS course, divides the subject into Assessment Objectives to test your knowledge of the ways that English Literature works, but these areas are very closely interrelated and sometimes overlap. In the final module in the course, Reading for Meaning, all the Assessment Objectives are tested, to show what you've learned about the study of English Literature during the whole Advanced Level course. In working through these three poems in this Introduction, you've done exactly that – you've read texts for meaning, using each of the Assessment Objectives to do it.

Module ④ Texts in Time

This module carries 30% of the final A2 mark and 15% of the final A Level mark. The marks are divided amongst the Assessment Objectives like this:

ASSESSMENT OBJECTIVES

AO1 communicate clearly the knowledge, understanding and insight appropriate to literary study, using appropriate terminology and accurate and coherent written expression
(6% of the final A2 mark; 3% of the final A Level mark)

AO2ii respond with knowledge and understanding to literary texts of different types and periods, exploring and commenting on relationships and comparisons between literary texts
(5% of the final A2 mark; 2.5% of the final A Level mark)

AO3 show detailed understanding of the ways in which writers' choices of form, structure and language shape meanings
(6% of the final A2 mark; 3% of the final A Level mark)

AO4 articulate independent opinions and judgements, informed by different interpretations of literary texts by other readers
(7% of the final A2 mark; 3.5% of the final A Level mark)

AO5ii evaluate the significance of cultural, historical and other contextual influences on literary texts and study
(6% of the final A2 mark; 3% of the final A Level mark)

All of the Assessment Objectives are tested in this module, and they are allocated to period/genre in the following ways:

- Both Section A, Drama Pre-1770 and Section B Poetry Pre-1900 target Assessment Objectives 1, 2 and 3.
- Section A targets the additional dominant AO4.
- Section B targets the additional dominant AO5ii.

The main emphasis for your studies will be the dominant Assessment Objective for each period/genre, although you should pay attention to the other Assessment Objectives as well.

Content

This module meets the core syllabus requirements for Drama Pre-1770 and Poetry Pre-1900.

The examination

The question paper is split into two sections, Section A, Drama Pre-1770 and Section B, Poetry Pre-1900. You need to answer one question from each section. The questions are weighted equally, and marks are scaled to achieve the final mark. You are *not* allowed to take your texts into the examination for this paper.

How your work is assessed

The examiner will make an initial appraisal of your answer by making a judgement on your response to the dominant Assessment Objective for each section (AO4 for Section A, and AO5ii for Section B). Then your response to the other three Assessment Objectives will be assessed. This will, in general, confirm your initial mark, but may raise or lower it.

This module is designed to revise and build upon the work you did and the skills you acquired in AS Level Module 3, Texts in Context. It might be helpful to remind yourself of the work you did for this earlier module, and of the critical vocabulary you have already acquired. You do not need to work through the whole of Section A, Drama Pre-1770, as you will concentrate only on the text which you are studying. Nor do you need to work through the whole of Section B, Poetry Pre-1900, as again you will be studying one text only. However, it could be helpful to read through all the questions for Module 4 in this book to appreciate the different ways in which the Romantic context may be presented in these tasks.

Assessment Objective 4

This objective is more complex at A2 Level than it was at AS Level. You will need to be aware that:

- texts are open to multiple interpretations
- interpretations can change over time
- different readers bring different individual, social and cultural experiences to the reading of texts.

In the examination you will be assessed equally in two areas:

1 Your grasp/consideration of the critical views which may be offered in a question

2 Your own individual response to and judgement on your text.

This means that you must have a thorough knowledge and understanding of your chosen play, be flexible enough to take on board other readers' experiences of the play, and be confident enough to express and justify your own responses to the play and to interpretations offered by others. In doing this, you will also fulfil Assessment Objectives 1, 2 and 3.

In the Specimen Units offered for AQA Specification A, there are seven different ways in which AO4 appears in the examination questions:

1 You are given two opposing critical views and asked to discuss these and other views. This creates an opportunity to offer your own opinions.

2 You are offered two opposing critical views and asked to explore these, and the play, further.

3 You are offered one critical view and asked if you agree or disagree, or have further views to add.

4 You are offered two critical views to evaluate, with a request for additional opinions.

5 You are offered one critical view to assess and asked if there are other ideas to consider as well.

6 You are offered two critical views and asked if you agree with one/both/neither.

7 You are given two critical views from different historical periods and asked how far you agree with these, and what other views there might be.

The examples given in the Specimen Units are not exhaustive, and there will be other ways of testing AO4:

- you may be given two similar or related views from different critics to support or to argue against

- you could be offered two critical views from different social/cultural groups and asked to evaluate these, and perhaps explore further the views offered.

What is important is that in all cases you carry out two tasks:

- assess the critical view(s) offered

- offer your own judgement/opinion as requested.

For each play below two sample tasks will be offered as a framework. Each of these will be based on key critical issues of the text. You may then develop these fully in your own time. In addition to these models, several further tasks will also be suggested, with an activity as a starting point, for you to work on yourself. These will also be based on central critical issues related to the text.

Othello by William Shakespeare

In *Othello* you see how Shakespeare explores the nature of the love between Othello and Desdemona, how people should or should not behave in society, and wider, universal matters of morality and religion.

In this section you will look at six different critical perspectives on *Othello*:

1 Whether *Othello* is anything more than an account of a personal tragedy.

2 The nature of audience response to the dramatic effects within the play.

3 Whether Desdemona is a victim or a temptress.

4 Whether Othello himself is a noble man.

5 Whether Iago is a devil, or just a jealous, scheming individual.

6 The idea that everything that is beautiful will decay and destroy itself.

1 *Othello* – a personal tragedy?

One critic has suggested that *Othello* lacks **universal** significance and is merely a story of terrible individual catastrophe. But another has written: 'Othello *is* the human soul as it strives to be and Iago *is* that which corrodes or subverts it from within.'

Examine each view and then indicate your own opinion on the play.

Try building your answer in three stages:

1 Consider the first criticism, that *Othello* is not a great tragedy because it is restricted to the personal problems of an individual.

2 Consider the second opinion that on the other hand there is a wide and universal look at the moral state of *all* mankind in this play.

3 You must be confident enough in your grasp of the text to present a viewpoint of your own. You could offer:

- agreement with one viewpoint or the other

- a compromise between both viewpoints

- outright rejection of these ideas

- a discussion of a viewpoint of your own.

Here is a sample response to this question, but remember that all interpretations are personal or subjective, that there is no single correct reading of any text, and that you should treat these points as a framework and expand on it in your own time.

In reply to the first critical comment, consider:

- the settings of the play

- the events of the play

- the characters of Iago and Othello generally.

Set against this would be a response to the second critical view:

- here you could focus on the imagery and the language used by individual characters.

The settings of the play

ACTIVITY 1

1 Make a list of the sequence of settings in *Othello*. What do you notice about these?

2 Work out the significance of the movement from Venice, the thriving seaport and centre of civilisation, to Cyprus, to a castle in Cyprus, to rooms in the castle, to a bedchamber, to the bed in this room. Does this suggest that *Othello* is a personal and domestic tragedy? Could Shakespeare have had any other reasons to make the settings progressively more domestic and intimate?

The events of the play

ACTIVITY 2

1 Summarise the events of the play.

2 What are the motivations behind these events?

3 Could these events be described as domestic or personal or trivial?

4 Could you see these events in another way?

Some consideration of Iago and Othello

To support a reading that this is a personal tragedy for Iago, without universal significance, consider Iago's motivation in the following speech in Act 1, Scene 1:

> One Michael Cassio, a Florentine,
> A fellow almost damn'd in a fair wife,
> That never set a squadron in the field, [. . .]
> He, in good time, must his lieutenant be,
> And I, God bless the mark, his worship's ancient.

ACTIVITY 3

1 What do you think Iago feels here? Why might he appear to be so put out?

2 What are all the reasons for his jealousy of Cassio?

3 What else do you learn about Iago here?

Iago eventually has another reason for disliking Othello, as you may see by reading Act 1, Scene 3 ('I hate the Moor [. . .]').

ACTIVITY 4

1 What do you think is Iago's second reason for hating Othello?

2 Where else is this idea repeated in the play?

3 Do you think that Iago's reasons are genuine or not?

4 What does Iago have to say about reputation in Act 3, Scene 3?

At times we are given a negative view of Othello. Look at the first scene of the play:

> [. . .] that your fair daughter,
> At this odd-even and dull watch o' the night,
> Transported with no worse nor better guard,
> But with a knave of common hire, a gondolier,
> To the gross clasps of a lascivious Moor: [. . .]

ACTIVITY 5

1 Has Othello treated Desdemona with proper respect, as the daughter of a wealthy Venetian? Does Othello have different attitudes and customs perhaps? Has he understood the social conventions of Venice?

2 Why does Shakespeare offer a contrast between 'fair' and 'Moor'?

3 Why does Shakespeare use the plural 'clasps'? What aspect of their relationship is stressed? What might this tell you about Iago's attitude?

ACTIVITY 6

Now look at the choice Othello makes when he is tempted by Iago in Act 3, Scene 3. Throughout the scene you see Othello changing his mind, until after the Cassio episode he declares:

All my fond love thus do I blow to heaven, . . .
'Tis gone.
Arise, black vengeance, from thy hollow cell, [. . .]

1 Why is Othello so easily swayed? Is he simply jealous?

2 Could it be that he does not know his wife at all? Or that he is not intelligent enough to understand her?

Finally, look closely at the characters within the play and their status. The Duke is noble, but what is his part in the play? Look at the status, or place in the **social hierarchy**, of Othello, Desdemona and Iago.

For all these reasons you could claim that the play is a domestic, personal tragedy. But there is also the other view, that the play is a universal demonstration of a battle between good and evil. Here you could offer as supporting evidence, the language used in the play, particularly the imagery.

Language and imagery

Iago is repeatedly linked to the devil:

Divinity of hell!
When devils will their blackest sins put on,
They do suggest at first with heavenly shows,
As I do now: [. . .]

(Act 2, Scene 3)

ACTIVITY 7

1 How does Iago align himself with the devil here?

2 How is an opposition set up between heaven and hell?

3 List and explore other **diabolical** references in Iago's words. Could he be a **vice figure** or devil as in a **morality play**?

(It might help to remind yourself of the discussion of *Dr Faustus* as a morality play in *AS English Literature for AQA A*, page 89.)

On the other hand, *Desdemona* is often associated with heaven (Act 5, Scene 2):

> Then heaven
> Have mercy on me!

ACTIVITY 8

1 How is Desdemona related to Christian virtue here?

2 Carefully list and explore religious references in Desdemona's other speeches. Do you see any negative aspects of Desdemona?

Many critics have commented on the change in Othello's language from the poetic imagery at the beginning of the play, to the point where he takes on Iago's language (as in Act 3, Scene 3, above). At the end of the play (Act 5, Scene 2) Othello realises what has happened and says:

> Will you, I pray, demand that demi-devil
> Why he hath thus ensnar'd my soul and body?

ACTIVITY 9

1 What sort of understanding do you think Othello has reached by this point?

2 How could it relate to a battle of good and evil over man's soul?

In *Othello* you can see evidence of the **seven deadly sins**: pride, covetousness, lust, gluttony (or drunkenness, as in the case of Cassio, for example), anger, envy, sloth.

ACTIVITY 10

Work out the ways in which these sins appear in *Othello*.

Other critics believe that when Iago ensnares Othello because of Desdemona, it is a reworking of Adam and Eve's **Fall from Paradise**:

> Now by heaven
> My blood begins my safer guides to rule
> And passion having my best judgement collied
> Assays to lead the way.
>
> (Act 2, Scene 3)

ACTIVITY 11

1 What exactly is Othello suggesting here?

2 Can you see any opposition between 'safe guidance' and 'passion'?

3 Think about the story of the Fall from Paradise – Adam fell into Satan's trap when he gave in to his passion for Eve. Is there any link with *Othello*?

These are the two critical positions for you to think about and choose between when considering this particular perspective on *Othello*. You must indicate your choice, and explain your response, or reject both and add another viewpoint.

2 The audience's response to the drama in *Othello*

It has been suggested that part of the greatness of *Othello* lies in the relentless and sustained grip on the emotions of the audience. What do you think is great about the dramatic art of *Othello*?

In response to this you could consider several aspects of the play:

- settings
- plot
- use of character
- use of language
- treatment of time.

Settings

You could refer to the notes about settings you made for the previous question.

ACTIVITY 12

1 What reason could Shakespeare have for narrowing down the settings to smaller and smaller spaces?

2 Is the audience distanced from, or drawn in to, the bedroom scene?

3 Is the relationship between audience and actors here intimate or distant?

Plot

ACTIVITY 13

Look at the sequence of events you worked out in Activity 2. Is the plot simple? Is there a sub-plot? What are the effects of this?

Use of character

ACTIVITY 14

1 Look at the first scene again.

   • How does Shakespeare build up to the introduction of Othello?

   • Does the audience have certain expectations about Othello?

   • How does his noble language affect you? Are you forced to rethink?

2 How many important speaking characters are there in the play?

3 What effect is produced by having so few?

Use of language

One of the language effects which increases the tension of the play is the use of repetition.

ACTIVITY 15

Remind yourself of two scenes: that between Iago and Roderigo in Act 1, Scene 2 with the repeated refrain 'put money in thy purse', and the confrontation between Othello and Emilia in Act 5, Scene 2 with the repeated 'husband'.

1 Why do you think Shakespeare uses this repetition?

2 How does it help to build up tension or affect the pace of the verse?

3 How does the prose style of the first scene reflect the theme?

4 Why does Shakespeare split the lines between the two speakers here?

Treatment of time

The action in *Othello* appears to move very quickly, with the action in Cyprus taking place in just thirty-six hours; this is known as the 'short time'. But Shakespeare has to present the idea that certain events, such as the journey from Venice to Cyprus, the interval in which Cassio is suspected of flirting with Desdemona, must naturally take longer than this – the 'long time'. Critics call this Shakespeare's use of 'double time'. Here are two examples:

> BIANCA   What, keep a week away? seven days and nights?
>
> (Act 3, Scene 4)
>
> EMILIA   My, wayward husband hath a hundred times
> Woo'd me to steal it, [. . .]
>
> (Act 3, Scene 3)

ACTIVITY 16

Make a list of the other places in the play where 'double time' can be seen.

1 Why do you think that Shakespeare uses this technique?

2 Are you aware as you watch the play that this is happening?

3 How could it help to keep the tension high?

In addition to these points, you may add some of your own. Or you could disagree with the premise, and argue that there is no suspense.

Suggestions for further tasks:

3 Desdemona – a victim or a temptress?

One critic has suggested that Desdemona suffers at the hands of a patriarchal, male-dominated society. Another thinks that she is a temptress. How far do you agree with one or other of these viewpoints?

ACTIVITY 17

You could begin by working out Desdemona's increasing isolation; and also the failure of her language as she uses song to express herself.

4 Is Othello a noble man?

Is Othello the 'noble Moor', or is he full of pride and egotism and without self-knowledge? Do you agree with these assessments or do you have a completely different opinion of Othello?

ACTIVITY 18

Trace Othello's early use of poetic language up to the temptation scene with Iago, then his decline into Iago's language, until he returns to his original manner of speech near the end of the play.

1 Is Othello's fault gullibility? Or is he an outsider to Venetian society?

2 Could this be part of the reason that he is presented as a black Moor?

5 Is Iago a devil?

Is Iago a devil as some critics suggest, or just a low-minded military man, as others believe? Evaluate these views, adding your own if you wish.

ACTIVITY 19

Iago seems to be caught out by his own plans, to be afraid at Othello's words 'Villain, be sure thou prove my love a whore, [. . .]' (Act 3, Scene 3).

• Does he lose control of events in the last act of the play?

6 All beauty must destroy itself eventually

A leading critic believes that Shakespeare expressed the view (later shared by Keats) that in *Othello* all beauty and happiness carries within it the seeds of its own destruction. Do you agree with this? Think of evidence from the play to support this view.

ACTIVITY 20

	If it were now to die,
OTHELLO	'Twere now to be most happy, [. . .]
	(Act 2, Scene 1)

DESDEMONA	But that our loves and comforts should increase,
	Even as our days do grow.
	(Act 2, Scene 1)

1 How perfect is their love at first? How well do they know each other?

2 How do one's ideas about love differ from the other's?

Now you have considered these six different perspectives on *Othello*, you can carry on to use this framework to explore other aspects of the play.

Henry IV Part 2 by William Shakespeare

Henry IV Part 2 is one of Shakespeare's history plays. Here, as in his other history plays, Shakespeare deals with the issues of kingship as they affect the nation, and also with the conflict these issues cause to the individual, Henry IV.

As in the previous section, you will look at critical perspectives on *Henry IV Part 2*.

1 How far the play is concerned with Hal's education as future king.

2 Whether Falstaff is a 'devil', or just good-humoured and lively.

3 Whether Hal is the pivot linking sub- and main plots together.

4 How far *Henry IV Part 2* can be seen as a history play, operating in a 'timeless sphere'.

5 To what extent *Henry IV Part 2* is a morality play.

6 Whether Falstaff is a corrupt and dangerous flatterer.

1 Hal's education as future king

'Hal is subjected to a process of education which finally allows him to assume with full competence the burden of authority created by his father's own act . . .'. Do you agree that this is the central idea in *Henry IV Part 2*?

First you need to consider the opinion expressed in the quotation. Then you have to offer your own opinion about this critical viewpoint.

The quotation can be broken down into two parts:

• Hal's father's own act

• Hal's education.

Then you need to decide how far you agree with this, and whether you think this summary misses out any other important elements of the play.

Hal's father's own act

This refers to Henry's usurpation of the crown. We see Henry worrying about this in Act 4, Scene 5:

> God knows, my son,
> By what by-paths and indirect crooked ways
> I met this crown, and I myself know well
> How troublesome it sat upon my head.

ACTIVITY 1

1 How does Henry feel about his way of gaining the crown? Why does he use the word 'met'?

2 Pick out words and phrases such as 'met', 'by-paths', 'indirect crooked ways'. What might these words suggest? Why are certain adjectives used?

3 Read the whole of this long speech, and look at the style it is written in. Is it formal? Or solemn? What effect does this have on you?

4 Look for other examples in the play where Henry reveals his thoughts.

Others are conscious of being treated badly by Henry IV. Morton relates the Archbishop of York's words to the English people in Act 1, Scene 1:

And doth enlarge his rising with the blood
Of fair King Richard, scraped from Pomfret stones;
Derives from Heaven his quarrel and his cause;
Tells them he doth bestride a bleeding land,
Gasping for life under great Bolingbroke, [. . .]

ACTIVITY 2

1 How does the Archbishop try to persuade the people? Which words are used emotively?

2 What might the word 'Heaven' signify? Could the word be a reference to Henry IV not having **'Divine Right'** because he usurped the crown by killing Richard?

3 Should the Archbishop, as Church leader, provoke rebellion?

4 How does Henry deal with the Archbishop later in the play?

Hal's education

Warwick explains (Act 4, Scene 4) why Hal mixes with the 'low-life' crowd of Eastcheap:

The prince but studies his companions
Like a strange tongue, wherein, to gain the language,
'Tis needful that the most immodest word
Be looked upon and learnt; [. . .]

ACTIVITY 3

1 What reasons does Warwick give for the prince's behaviour?

2 How does Warwick view the Eastcheap crowd?

3 What do you think Hal could gain from mixing with these people?

Hal himself seems ready to make the break and take on his kingly role:

> By heaven, Poins, I feel me much to blame
> So idly to profane the precious time,
> When tempest of commotion, like the south,
> Borne with black vapour, doth begin to melt
> And drop upon our bare unarmèd heads.
>
> (Act 2, Scene 4)

ACTIVITY 4

1 What are Hal's feelings here? Is Poins used to reveal these feelings?

2 How does the language intensify these feelings?

3 Look back at the scene between Hal and Poins in Act 2, Scene 2. How does Shakespeare use Poins in the play?

When Hal becomes Henry V, after the death of his father, he switches his choice of 'tutor' from Falstaff to the Lord Chief Justice:

> For which, I do commit into your hand
> Th'unstainèd sword that you have used to bear, [. . .]
> You shall be as a father to my youth, [. . .]
>
> (Act 5, Scene 2)

ACTIVITY 5

1 How do these words reflect the change of adviser from Falstaff to Lord Chief Justice?

2 What significance does this handing over of responsibility for justice and judgement have for the monarchy?

3 What is the significance of the word 'unstainèd'?

Finally, Henry V is confronted by his former companion Falstaff and rejects him:

I know thee not, old man. Fall to thy prayers.
How ill white hairs become a fool and jester!
I have long dreamt of such a kind of man,
So surfeit-swell'd, so old and so profane, [. . .]

(Act 5, Scene 5)

ACTIVITY 6

1   What is Henry's attitude to Falstaff now? Do you think he is critical?

2   Why does Henry refer to 'prayers' and use the word 'profane'? Could there be a reference to morality in these words?

3   Do you find Henry V just or cold in this scene? Why?

4   Could such references have other significance in the play's overall framework?

This then, is a brief outline of a possible response to the first two parts of the question which you could develop later. You would still need to address the question of whether you think this is the central idea of the play.

2 Falstaff – a 'devil' or just a good-humoured old man

Some critics see Falstaff as a devil, leading Hal into bad ways. Others suggest that he deserves some sympathy, for he has simply 'exuberance of good humour and good nature'. Assessing both of these views, how do you respond to Falstaff?

In response to this you could consider:

• Falstaff as a 'devil', leading Hal astray

• a more sympathetic view of Falstaff.

Finally, you must offer an opinion of your own.

Is Falstaff a devil?

Some critics see Falstaff as a vice figure from a morality play, the Lord of Misrule, of Rioting and of Feast. Falstaff is often seen drinking sack and eating great feasts.

In Act 1, Scene 2 the Lord Chief Justice speaks to him:

CH. JUST.	You have misled the youthful prince.
FALSTAFF	The young prince hath misled me. I am the fellow with the great belly, and he my dog. [. . .]
CH. JUST.	You follow the young prince up and down, like his ill angel.

ACTIVITY 7

1 What is the Lord Chief Justice accusing Falstaff of here?

2 What is Falstaff's defence to this?

3 Explore the significance of the phrase 'ill angel'. (In a traditional morality play, the main character was accompanied by a good and a bad angel or spirit. You may refer to the discussion of the morality play in *AS English Literature for AQA A*, page 89.)

4 Falstaff's fatness is stressed here; the prince is often referred to as thin or lean. Look at other examples of these sorts of descriptions. What do they suggest?

In Act 5, Scene 5 Hal as Henry V rejects Falstaff:

When thou dost hear I am as I have been,
Approach me, and thou shall be as thou wast,
The tutor and the feeder of my riots; [. . .]

ACTIVITY 8

1 What is Hal's attitude to Falstaff now?

2 How does he see his past relationship with Falstaff?

Other critics see Falstaff as even more dangerous than this. In Act 1, Scene 2 we see Falstaff intending to take advantage of the rebel wars:

A good wit will make use of anything: I will turn diseases to commodity.

ACTIVITY 9

1 What are the 'diseases' of the land he refers to?

2 Explore the imagery of disease and purification in the rest of the play. What is its significance?

3 What is Falstaff's attitude here? Is it loyal? Or worthy? Or selfish?

Look also at Falstaff's attitude when he hears of Henry's accession to the throne in Act 5, Scene 3:

I know the young King is sick for me. Let us take any man's horses, the laws of England are at my commandment. Blessed are they that have been my friends, and woe to my Lord Chief Justice!

ACTIVITY 10

1 What does Falstaff think about his own position now?

2 Does he have any right to think that he can manipulate the law to suit himself?

3 Who does he see as his greatest enemy here?

4 Do you think that Falstaff could represent the breakdown of law in society?

Falstaff shows an exuberance of good humour and good nature

You could use the Boar's Head Tavern scenes with their rowdy humour to support this view, using as evidence the tricks Hal plays on Falstaff, the comedy created here, and the sense of friendliness. As Falstaff says (Act 5, Scene 1):

I will devise matter enough out of this Shallow to keep Prince Harry in continual laughter the wearing out of six fashions – [. . .]

ACTIVITY 11

1 What attitude does Falstaff adopt towards Hal here?

2 How does Falstaff see his role?

3 How do you see his role in the play?

Falstaff seems to know his prince and thinks that he has helped him (Act 4, Scene 3):

[. . .] for the cold blood he did naturally inherit of his father he hath, like lean, sterile and bare land, manured, husbanded and tilled, with excellent endeavour of drinking good and good store of fertile sherris, [. . .]

ACTIVITY 12

1 What does Falstaff think of Hal?

2 Could Falstaff have a valid point about coldness, leisure and friendship?

3 Do you think that Falstaff has any value as a commentator?

You could develop this positive aspect of Falstaff. Here are some of his words to the newly crowned Henry V, and to his friends (Act 5, Scene 5):

God save thy grace, King Hal! my royal Hal! [. . .]

God save thee, my sweet boy! [. . .]

[. . .] Do not you grieve at this. I shall be sent for in private to him;

ACTIVITY 13

1 What are Falstaff's feelings for Hal? What do you feel for Falstaff?

2 Can Falstaff perhaps be seen as part of an old order, a sick old knight now out of date in the kingdom of Henry V?

The activities and comments above offer an outline for your response to both critical viewpoints. To complete the task, you should now make your own position about Falstaff clear.

Suggestions for further tasks:

3 Hal as the pivot, linking sub- and main plots

It has been suggested that Hal is the technical centre of the play, linking the two levels, the 'high life' and the 'low life'. How far do you agree with this judgement?

ACTIVITY 14

Begin by working out the parallel actions in the play, for example the meeting with the rebels in Act 2, Scene 3 is followed immediately by the quarrel at the Boar's Head. What might be the purposes of this structure?

4 *Henry IV Part 2* as a history play but existing in a 'timeless sphere'

One critic believes that a history play 'largely operates in a timeless sphere'. How far is this true of *Henry IV Part 2*?

ACTIVITY 15

Look at Warwick's words in Act 3, Scene 1: 'There is a history in all men's lives [. . .]' Do you agree that the history plays set out to show that history repeats itself? Is this part of their value?

5 *Henry IV Part 2* as a morality play

'*Henry IV Part 2* is a morality play, whose main theme is the growing up of a madcap prince into the ideal king.' Do you agree with this statement?

ACTIVITY 16

You could start by looking at how this play uses some of the conventions of the morality play. Which characters are partly allegorical? Think about the names and functions of characters such as Rumour, Wart and Mould.

6 Falstaff – a corrupt and dangerous flatterer?

One critic has said of Falstaff: 'We have considered him . . . too seriously in that we hold him in the balance against Henry and England, and too lightly in that as a corrupt flatterer he stands for the overthrow of divinely ordained political order.' Bearing this assessment in mind, what is your own view of Falstaff?

You could begin by examining the king's words from Act 4, Scene 5:

For the fifth Harry from curbed licence plucks
The muzzle of restraint, and the wild dog
Shall flesh his tooth on every innocent.

ACTIVITY 17

1 Look closely at the harsh language used here. Why is it so strong?

2 Look at the image of the dog: what is the significance of this?

3 What is your response to this serious accusation?

4 What would England be like if it were full of people like Falstaff?

Having studied these six aspects of *Henry IV Part 2*, you can now use this framework to explore other aspects of the play.

The Merchant of Venice by William Shakespeare

In this play – a comedy with serious overtones – Shakespeare looks at how people behave as individuals and lovers, in the ways they conduct their daily business, and at people as members of a satisfactory, well-functioning society.

In this section you will look at six critical perspectives on *The Merchant of Venice*:

1 The idea that there are three clear phases in Shakespearean comedy.

2 Whether Shylock deserves some sympathy or is unnaturally cruel.

3 Whether Portia may be seen to embody the values of the play.

4 Whether Antonio and Shylock represent opposite poles in the play.

5 Whether there is a conflict between Old Testament and New Testament law.

6 Whether the values of Venice and Belmont are seen to be in conflict.

1 Three phases of a Shakespearean comedy

It has been suggested that there are three phases in a Shakespearean comedy. The first phase is that of an unsettled society governed by a harsh or irrational law; the second phase is that of temporarily lost identity, and the third phase is the discovery of identity and reconciliation. How far do you think that this can be applied to *The Merchant of Venice*?

Look at each of the three suggested phases in turn, and then make your own final judgement.

An unsettled society governed by a harsh or irrational law

You could start by looking at the role of usury in society, which becomes clear in Shylock's exchanges with Bassanio and Antonio in Act 1, Scene 3:

> I hate him for he is a Christian:
> But more, for that in low simplicity
> He lends out money gratis, and brings down
> The rate of usance here with us in Venice [. . .]

Later Shylock comments:

> [. . .] you neither lend nor borrow
> Upon advantage.
>
> (Act 1, Scene 3)

Antonio replies:

> I do never use it.
>
> (Act 1, Scene 3)

ACTIVITY 1

1 What is Shylock's 'profession', and his attitude towards it?

2 How does Bassanio compare with Shylock over this matter of money-lending?

3 Is Shylock's role as usurer legal in Venice? Do you think that there may be something wrong with Venetian law, bearing in mind that later the Duke has to support Shylock's *legal* bond?

People in this society seem gloomy, first Antonio and then Portia:

> In sooth I know not why I am so sad,
> It wearies me, you say it wearies you;
>
> (Act 1, Scene 1)
>
> By my troth Nerissa, my little body is aweary of this great world.
>
> (Act 1, Scene 2)

ACTIVITY 2

1 What sort of mood is created by Antonio's words at the start of the play? How do Portia's words develop this effect?

2 Is this the sort of mood you would normally associate with comedy?

3 Has this mood changed by the end of the play?

Temporarily lost identity

Portia tells Nerissa of the plan to go to court in disguise (Act 3, Scene 4):

PORTIA	[. . .] we'll see our husbands Before they think of us!
NERISSA	Shall they see us?
PORTIA	They shall Nerissa: but in such a habit, That they shall think we are accomplished With that we lack; [. . .]

ACTIVITY 3

1 Do you think their disguises are realistic enough to fool their lovers?

2 Could these disguises be hinting at confusion about other things, such as the real value of love, or the law, or gender or personal identity?

In the court scene at Venice (Act 4, Scene 1), the law is the subject of scrutiny (and of 'lost identity'), and the theme of mercy is introduced. The Duke addresses Shylock, expecting him to forgo his bond:

[. . .] and then 'tis thought
Thou'lt show thy mercy and remorse more strange
Than is thy strange apparent cruelty;
And where thou now exacts the penalty, [. . .]

ACTIVITY 4

1 What is the Duke's attitude to Shylock as a fellow human being?

2 What is the Duke's attitude as protector of the law of Venice here and elsewhere in the play? Antonio says 'The Duke cannot deny the course of law' (Act 3, Scene 3).

3 Does this ambiguity mean that the law could in some way support murder?

Now re-read Portia's 'mercy' speech (Act 4, Scene 1).

4 What is the importance of showing mercy?

5 Would the idea of justice be made more acceptable if it included mercy?

6 Could the Christians, as well as Shylock, learn from these ideas?

Think about what Portia is suggesting here – the defeat of the spirit of **legalism** in favour of a more enlightened and charitable society. Do you agree with her?

The discovery of identity and reconciliation

The final scene of the play (Act 5, Scene 1) is at Belmont, in moonlight. Music adds to Lorenzo's words, which suggests that harmony has been achieved:

[. . .] soft stillness and the night
Become the touches of sweet harmony: [. . .]

Such harmony is in immortal souls, [. . .]

ACTIVITY 5

1 Do you think that these words hint at a perfect society?

2 Does Shakespeare suggest that humans can achieve this state of harmony?

Hearing the music, Lorenzo continues (Act 5, Scene 1):

The man that hath no music in himself,
Nor is not moved with concord of sweet sounds,
Is fit for treasons, stratagems, and spoils, [. . .]

ACTIVITY 6

1 Which words convey a sense of harmony and of peace? How do they do this?

2 Look back to Act 2, Scene 5. What was Shylock's attitude to music there?

3 Where is Shylock at the end of the play?

4 Why do you think that he has been excluded from this 'new' society?

The play ends with the lovers restating their vows, the business of the rings between Portia and Bassanio, the revealing of Portia's and Nerissa's disguises and Gratiano's final words (Act 5, Scene 1):

Well, while I live, I'll fear no other thing
So sore, as keeping safe Nerissa's ring.

ACTIVITY 7

Look out all the references to the word 'ring' and the different meanings. Think about:

• the ring of harmony of the stars

• the ring as an emblem of harmony between two people in love

• the ring as an indication of possession, protection and of sexuality.

Remember, this is a brief outline of a possible response to the question about the 'three-phase' theory which you could develop later. To complete your answer to this question you should now consider how far you think that the statement on page 21 is valid for *The Merchant of Venice*, and whether you would like to add any other points.

2 Does Shylock deserve some sympathy?

'Our sympathies are much oftener with Shylock than with his enemies.'

'Shylock was unnatural in his cruelty.'

Consider these two comments, and give your own view of Shylock.

We often have more sympathy with Shylock than with his enemies

Supporters of Shylock often refer to his 'many a time and oft' speech in Act 1, Scene 3:

> What should I say to you? Should I not say
> 'Hath a dog money? is it possible
> A cur can lend three thousand ducats?' or
> Shall I bend low, [. . .]

ACTIVITY 8

1 How does Shakespeare gain sympathy for Shylock here and elsewhere in this long speech?

2 What is Antonio's attitude to Shylock? Does he have genuine reasons for disliking him?

3 Do you actually see Antonio behaving badly towards Shylock?

4 Do you ever see Shylock alone on stage, to **soliloquise** to the audience?

5 Does Shylock change his view towards the 'Christian' group?

Later in the play (Act 3, Scene 1) Shylock is given another moving speech:

> Hath not a Jew eyes? hath not a Jew hands, organs, dimensions, senses, affections, passions? fed with the same food, hurt with the same weapons, [. . .]

ACTIVITY 9

1 How does this speech make you feel?

2 How does the style of the speech contribute to its effect?

Shakespeare manipulates this response soon afterwards when Tubal enters and announces the elopement of Jessica, Shylock's only daughter:

> I would my daughter were dead at my foot, and the jewels in her ear: would she were hears'd at my foot, and the ducats in her coffin: [. . .]

ACTIVITY 10

1 In the light of the previous extract from earlier in the scene, how does this speech make you feel about Shylock now?

2 What does Shylock regret? What kind of attitude does he show towards his daughter?

3 Does he show any qualities which you would associate with a father?

Shylock is unnatural in his cruelty

Later in Act 3, Antonio talks about Shylock to Solanio:

> I oft deliver'd from his forfeitures
> Many that have at times made moan to me,
> Therefore he hates me.
>
> (Act 3, Scene 3)

ACTIVITY 11

1 Why does Antonio think that Shylock hates him?

2 What effect has Shylock had on the lives of these people who borrowed from him?

You have already seen some evidence of Shylock's attitude towards Jessica. She herself says in Act 2, Scene 3: 'Our house is hell.'

ACTIVITY 12

1 Why does Jessica think that her home is 'hell'?

2 Look for the references to hell and the devil applied to Shylock by other characters. What do you think that these references imply?

Then there is the evidence of the trial itself. Shylock speaks to the Duke (Act 4, Scene 1):

You'll ask me why I rather choose to have
A weight of carrion flesh, than to receive
Three thousand ducats: I'll not answer that!

ACTIVITY 13

1 What do you think are Shylock's deeper motives here?

2 What is his attitude to the value of a human life?

3 What would the world be like if Shylock's values were the norm?

4 What sort of state and laws would exist, if they were governed by a world-view like Shylock's?

To complete the task, you should make your own opinion of Shylock clear.

3 The character 'Portia' embodies the values of the play

To respond to this statement, you could discuss Portia's 'mercy' speech, which was referred to in the first perspective discussed on page 23. In addition, you could consider Portia's words in Act 5, Scene 1, when she talks of the man who holds her ring: 'I will become as liberal as you, [. . .]'.

ACTIVITY 14

1 Do you feel, as some critics do, that Portia embodies the values of the play? How do you respond to her?

2 Has Portia herself learned something about the nature of love during the course of the play?

3 Do you think Portia, like the others, has had to change a little?

4 Antonio and Shylock represent opposite poles in the play?

Some critics see in Antonio and Shylock 'the two opposed poles of the play'. How far do you agree with this judgement?

You have already looked at Shylock's character in the second perspective, and have considered his attitudes as a usurer and towards other members of society. Critics see Antonio as the opposite to Shylock in these respects, including his nobility of spirit in his friendship with Bassanio, as seen in the letter sent to Belmont in Act 3, Scene 2: 'Sweet Bassanio, [. . .]'.

ACTIVITY 15

1   What is Antonio's attitude to Bassanio here? Is there any blame? Or regret?

Other critics see Antonio, like Shylock, as isolated in society. Consider now Antonio's character and situation in the play.

2   How strong is Antonio's love for Bassanio?

3   Why do you think Antonio is both 'in' and 'out' of the social harmony at the end of the play?

4   Could Antonio be seen as the true tragic figure in this play?

5 Is there a conflict between Old and New Testament laws?

Some critics see the play as a representation of 'Justice and Mercy, of the Old Law and the New'. How far do you agree with this judgement?

You have already looked at ideas of mercy and justice in this section. A useful starting point for this question could be the dilemma which the state of Venice is in over the trial. Look at Act 3, Scene 3, where Antonio talks of the bond: 'The duke cannot deny the course of law: [. . .]'.

ACTIVITY 16

1   How do you think Shakespeare resolves this dilemma?

2   Is the 'message' of the play that it is unwise to live by the letter of the law? Is it better to live by the charitable spirit of the law?

6 Is there a conflict between the values of Venice and Belmont?

Many critics see a central contrast between the values of Venice and of Belmont. Do you agree with this interpretation?

You could take as your starting point the similarity of language between the lovers and those involved in trade or commerce. For example, Bassanio's words when he describes Portia, who comes from Belmont, in Act 1, Scene 1: '[. . .] and her sunny locks [. . .]'.

ACTIVITY 17

1   Do you think there is an overlap between the values of Venice and those of Belmont?

2   How does Shakespeare link the words of love with those of trade?

3   Explore the lovers' language elsewhere to see where the ideas of trade and love overlap. What are the effects of this overlap?

Having examined the six critical perspectives, you can now use this framework to explore other aspects of the play.

Noah and His Sons, The Second Shepherds' Play, Herod the Great from The Complete Works of the Wakefield Master

The Mystery plays

The name of these plays comes from the French word *mystère*, meaning a craft. The name came about because the local medieval craft Guilds each took responsibility for putting on one of the plays in the cycle. The play chosen by each Guild was often related to their particular skill or craft, for example the shipwrights or the fishermen and sailors would be responsible for the production of *Noah and His Sons*.

Background and origins

Medieval society in Europe was Roman Catholic, and that is where the roots of the Mystery plays lie. In 1269, Pope Urban IV announced that the Church did not adequately celebrate the feast of the Eucharist. In 1313, Pope Clement V acted on these words and declared that a new feast would take place on the first Thursday after Trinity Sunday, to be known as Corpus Christi, the body of Christ. The purpose of the feast was to give thanks for man's salvation, and for the gift of the Eucharist. To celebrate the Eucharist properly, there had to be a contextualisation, setting the idea of Holy Communion within the whole sphere of Christian belief, and so the Mystery plays came into being. They dramatised this full history, from the Fall from Paradise, through Christ's Harrowing in Hell and Crucifixion, and the Last Judgement, preparing for the gift of the Eucharist. Since the plays covered the whole of mankind's moral history, they were performed in cycles, and took place in York, Wakefield, Chester, Coventry and Cornwall. Other cycles may have existed, but records are lost.

ACTIVITY 1

- As these plays are so closely linked to religious and biblical events, try to find out as much as you can about the key events in the Bible as background to the play.

- Because medieval society was Roman Catholic, research Catholic beliefs, particularly where they relate to the three texts you are studying.

Performance

Although Church officials decided on the source material for these plays, they were written locally, and it was left to the Guilds to work out how they were to be performed. The Guilds were jealous of each other, and each wanted to put on the best show, so a great deal of money was spent on elaborate stage machinery, pageant wagons and costumes.

The pageant wagons were decorated with elaborate scenery and were known as 'mansions' or 'houses'. They would travel around the town and stop in a semi-circle or straight line to perform the plays. Stages were also elaborate, often with two levels for acting. Hell might be represented by a huge dragon's head, for example, with the actors dressed as devils coming out of the mouth.

ACTIVITY 2

Discuss how the three plays might be staged – they will be very different from modern drama. It is known, for example, that for *The Second Shepherds' Play* there were two huts with a space between which was 'Palestine'. This might have been performed on two levels, with the stage platform representing the sea.

Audience

We know that the trade Guilds marched in procession, perhaps carrying the Host, or consecrated bread. In the course of the procession the plays would be performed. It was a huge festive occasion, with all the local population joining in to celebrate the strong faith which they all shared. Even so, the audience was quite sophisticated, and would be aware that the production was not naturalistic. They saw the actors both as local people whom they knew, and also as the biblical figures they portrayed on stage. In the same way, they saw the settings as representative both of the original setting from the Bible, and of the local area.

ACTIVITY 3

Looking at all three plays, discuss where the 'double-think' about settings might occur. For example, in *The Second Shepherds' Play*, the settings might suggest Palestine, but it was also important they were recognisably those of Wakefield. What is the effect of this?

Interpretations

Critical interpretations of these plays tend to be very different from those of later texts. Because the purpose and meaning of the plays are clear-cut, there are no other interpretations open for discussion. Instead, you should concentrate on other topics for discussion, such as:

- literary merit
- variety of style
- methods and effects of staging
- ways in which the plays engaged the audiences of the time
- reasons why the plays may still appeal to a modern audience
- the effectiveness of the plays in achieving their purposes.

This list is not exhaustive, but may help as a starting point.

Here, as in previous sections, you will look at six critical perspectives on these Mystery plays:

1 The effects created by the two narratives in *The Second Shepherds' Play*.

2 How the play *Noah and His Sons* is made appealing and significant to the audience of its time.

3 Why *Herod the Great* is considered to be such a dramatically effective play.

4 What the effects might be on people participating in a Mystery play.

5 Why the Mystery plays still appeal to a modern audience.

6 The nature of the humour in the Mystery plays.

1 What effects are created by the two nativities in *The Second Shepherds' Play*?

In the first nativity, Coll, Gib and Daw go to Mak's home about the sheep-stealing. They think at first a new baby has been born, until they begin to have doubts when Daw goes near (lines 549 ff.):

> [*But as he approaches the cradle and sniffs the air, he makes a grimace.*]
> Yet live cattle, as I may have bliss, nor tame nor wild,
> None has smelled so strong as this – this child! [. . .]
>
> What the devil is this? He has a long snout!

Then there is the second, or real nativity, when the shepherds approach the Christ child, offering their own sort of gifts. Gib goes to the child (lines 724–6):

> Hail, I kneel and I cower. – A bird have I brought
>   Without mar.
> Hail, little, tiny mop, [. . .]

ACTIVITY 4

1 Why do you think that there is a parody of the real nativity?

2 How does the second nativity – with the homely language and homely gifts – make you feel?

3 Do you think that this makes the play sincere, and relevant to its local audience?

2 How is the play *Noah and His Sons* made appealing and significant to the audience of its time?

Think about the familiar and funny domestic setting of the play; Noah has a nagging wife and they often quarrel (lines 211–12):

NOAH   Hold thy tongue, ram-skit, or I shall make thee still.

WIFE   By my thrift, if thou smite, I shall set on thee too.

ACTIVITY 5

1 Do you think this scene will seem familiar to much of the audience?

2 What do you think are the effects on the audience of presenting the religious content in such homely terms?

3 The Wakefield Master has also written in asides for the speakers to address the audience, for example, 'We women may curse all ill husbands' (line 205). What do you think the effects of these asides would have been?

3 Why is *Herod the Great* considered to be such a dramatically effective play?

If you have attended a performance of the Mystery plays, perhaps at Chester or at York, you will understand the powerful effect these plays still have on a modern audience. At a recent performance at York, some members of the audience were overtaken during the interval by the Devil, tail over arm, rushing out for a cool drink. (During performances, actors often did mingle with the audience.) The stage directions in *Herod the Great* read: 'HEROD raves on the street and in the pageant'. Here, the 'pageant' means the attending crowd. So the actor playing Herod would continue his performance in the midst of the spectators, and draw them into the action as participators.

ACTIVITY 6

1 Look at the twists and turns of Herod's argument. Work out how he trips himself up as he argues.

2 Do you think that Herod would have great stage presence?

3 Do you think that Herod might remind the audience how they themselves have argued their way out of a tight corner?

4 Is this play is a great dramatic contrast to the others? In what ways?

4 What effects might participating in these Mystery plays have on people?

ACTIVITY 7

1 What might an actor's motives have been in the Middle Ages? Would they be different today?

2 How do you think people would have reacted when a family member or friend took on one of these arduous parts?

3 Do you think that performing in one of these plays would increase a person's respect for God and religious ceremonies?

4 Do you think it might make a person realise that all ordinary people are capable of noble or wicked deeds?

5 How far do you think these aspects hold true today?

5 Why might the Mystery plays still appeal to a modern audience?

ACTIVITY 8

Think about the skills required in the writing of these plays, such as the deliberate anachronisms, the localisation of settings, the domestic situations, the asides to the audience, the use of references familiar to the audience, the humour and the overall complexity of the plays. Find evidence from all three plays here.

6 What do you make of the humour in the Mystery plays?

ACTIVITY 9

Think about and look for evidence of the different kinds of humour:

- savage knockabout farce
- irony, as in *Herod the Great*
- humour of situation, as in the two nativities
- humour of character.

Then assess how these various types of humour make the plays effective.

Now you have explored the six critical perspectives here, you can use this model to study other aspects on your own.

The Duchess of Malfi by John Webster

The Duchess of Malfi falls within the genre of revenge plays. The Elizabethan/Jacobean audience had mixed views about revenge, and an ambiguous attitude towards those who extracted it. While it was acceptable to avenge a murder of a blood-relative, or a very brutal murder, it was still an offence in the eyes of God to kill a fellow human being.

Revenge plays had certain characteristics: there would be one or more revengers; they were often set in Italy or Spain; there was often a discontented character who acted as commentator; there was intrigue, poisoning, violent actions and death; disguise was often used to create confusion, and there was a violent final scene. If you are asked to consider *The Duchess of Malfi* as a revenge play, these are the features you should discuss.

Below, you will look at six different critical perspectives on *The Duchess of Malfi*:

1 Whether there is evidence of a firm social and moral viewpoint.

2 How far the men are ruled by their intelligence or by their passions.

3 Whether it is only by their actions that characteristics are revealed.

4 How you respond to Bosola.

5 Whether there is any light in the darkness of the play.

6 Whether Webster presents his characters with pity or contempt.

1 Social and moral viewpoint

It has been commented that 'In *The Duchess of Malfi* there is an easily identifiable social and moral viewpoint against which to judge each of the characters'. How far do you agree with this judgement?

To answer this, you need to decide whether the statement is true, and/or offer another viewpoint. You could begin by looking at the speech of three of the characters: Antonio, Bosola and the Duchess.

Antonio

In Act 1, Scene 1, Antonio speaks about Ferdinand and the Cardinal, and then the Duchess:

> [. . .] and verily I believe them;
> For the devil speaks in them.
> But for their sister, the right noble duchess – [. . .]
> There speaketh so divine a continence
> As cuts off all lascivious, and vain hope.

ACTIVITY 1

1 Pick out the references that show the contrast between the brothers and the Duchess.

2 What do you understand about the Duchess from this speech?

3 At this point, what is Antonio's relationship with the Duchess?

Bosola

Bosola is also seen to be a reliable commentator by many critics. He describes the state of the nation under the rule of the brothers later in the same scene:

> He, and his brother, are like plum-trees, that grow
> crooked over standing pools; they are rich, and o'erladen
> with fruit, but none but crows, pies, and caterpillars feed
> on them: [. . .]

ACTIVITY 2

1 What is Bosola saying here about the brothers and their method of rule?

2 What images are used to create the effect? Where else are similar images used in the play?

3 How reliable a commentator do you think Bosola is?

The Duchess

The Duchess is fearless in the face of death, and critics point to her 'diamond' speech to show her contempt for her executioners (Act 4, Scene 2). She continues:

> Yet stay; heaven-gates are not so highly arch'd
> As princes' palaces, they that enter there
> Must go upon their knees. – [*Kneels*]

ACTIVITY 3

1 What is the Duchess's attitude to her brothers?

2 What is her attitude to death? Might this suggest her goodness?

3 How do you respond to the Duchess at the moment of her death?

If you take the speeches of Antonio and Bosola above, and the words and actions of the Duchess, you might agree that a social and moral judgement is being made. But many critics argue that Webster is not at all clear-cut in his attitude to traditional Christian attitudes to death.

The Cardinal says 'I am puzzled in a question about hell' (Act 5, Scene 5) and when he dies Bosola, despite his goodness in avenging the death of the Duchess, says:

> O, this gloomy world!
> In what a shadow, or deep pit of darkness,
> Doth womanish and fearful mankind live! [. . .]
> Mine is another voyage.
>
> (Act 5, Scene 5)

ACTIVITY 4

1 Why is the Cardinal, a churchman, puzzled about hell?

2 If there is a traditional Christianity, why does Bosola speak like this?

3 Do you think that there is any traditional Christian consolation at the end of the play?

2 Are men ruled by their intelligence or their passions?

One critic believes that in Jacobean drama the men are ruled by either their intelligence or their passions. Other critics argue that it is the absence of a motive that makes the Duchess's death so terrifying. What do you think about the brothers and their motivation?

Assess the first statement, and then relate it to the second, finally expressing your own opinion.

This time you could examine the three characters: Ferdinand, the Cardinal and Bosola. You could argue that Ferdinand is ruled by passion, the Cardinal by intelligence, and Bosola by a combination of the two.

Ferdinand

Ferdinand speaks to the Cardinal about the birth of his sister's child in Act 2, Scene 5:

> I have this night digg'd up a mandrake. [. . .]
>
> And I am grown mad with't. [. . .]

Read there – a sister damn'd; she's loose i'th'hilts': [. . .]

Till I know who leaps my sister, I'll not stir.

ACTIVITY 5

1 How does Ferdinand react to the news of the birth?

2 What sort of language does he use here and elsewhere in this scene?

3 Look for this combination of horror, violence and sex in Ferdinand's other speeches. What does it tell you about Ferdinand's state of mind and his obsessions?

4 Would you say that Ferdinand is ruled by intelligence or the passions?

The Cardinal

The Cardinal reacts sharply to Ferdinand's lack of control (Act 2, Scene 5):

CARD.   How idly shows this rage! which carries you,
        As men convey'd by witches through the air,
        On violent whirlwinds – this intemperate noise [. . .]

FERD.   Have not you
        My palsy?

CARD.   Yes – I can be angry
        Without this rupture: [. . .]
              – chide yourself.

ACTIVITY 6

1 What differences can you see in the temperaments of the two brothers?

2 Who do you think is the more controlled of the two? And the more dangerous?

3 What do you learn about the Cardinal's values here?

4 Would you say that the Cardinal is ruled by his intelligence?

Bosola

It could be claimed that initially Bosola is governed by a sort of passion. Here he speaks heatedly to Ferdinand:

I would have you curse yourself now, that your bounty,
Which makes men truly noble, e'er should make
Me a villain: [. . .]

(Act 1, Scene 1)

ACTIVITY 7

1   What is Bosola's relationship to the brothers? How does he serve them?

2   To what degree is he driven by the need for payment?

3   How aware is he of his own motives and wickedness?

4   Would you say he was ruled by both passion for money *and* intelligence? How do these two passions dictate his actions later in the play?

Now turn to the second part of the question, and the comment that 'it is the absence of a motive that makes the Duchess's death so terrifying'.

Many critics say that it is difficult to pin down the motives of the brothers. Early on in Act 1, Scene 1, the Cardinal hints at a motive when he talks to the Duchess about her marrying again:

No, nor anything without the addition, honour,
Sway your high blood.

Later he says (Act 2, Scene 5):

Shall our blood,
The royal blood of Arragon and Castile,
Be thus attainted?

ACTIVITY 8

1   What are the Cardinal's declared motives?

2   Look at his speech in Act 2, Scene 5. How important are appearances to him?

3   Do you think that he might have any other motives?

Ferdinand is often considered to be more complex. You have already looked at his passion for his sister, which he frequently declares, for example when he talks of 'her delicate skin', and adds 'Damn her! That body of hers', in Act 4, Scene 1.

ACTIVITY 9

What might these comments suggest about the nature of Ferdinand's feelings?

There is also another possible motive revealed in the exchange between Ferdinand and the Cardinal (Act 2, Scene 5):

> I could kill her now,
> In you, or in myself, for I do think
> It is some sin in us, heaven doth revenge
> By her.

ACTIVITY 10

1 What effect does the Duchess have on Ferdinand?

2 Might the Duchess's goodness make the brothers aware of their own evil and of their punishment to come?

Both motives seem to come together in Ferdinand's last speech (Act 5, Scene 5):

> My sister! O! my sister! there's the cause on't:
> *Whether we fall by ambition, blood, or lust,*
> *Like diamonds, we are cut with our own dust.*

ACTIVITY 11

1 Is it being suggested here that Ferdinand is his worst own enemy?

2 Does Webster deliberately make Ferdinand's motivation ambiguous and complex? Why?

Finally, you must make your own assessment of the characters of Ferdinand, the Cardinal and Bosola, and whether you think there are clear motives behind their actions. Consider as well the possibility that Webster makes his characters complex and ambiguous to deliberately unsettle or confuse the audience.

3 Characters are revealed only by their actions

It has been said that in *The Duchess of Malfi* 'it is only in action that men are truly themselves.' Do you agree with this assessment?

You have already looked at the difficulty of relating words to deeds with regard to the motives of Ferdinand and the Cardinal. It might be useful also to consider

Antonio, whom many critics find hard to assess. Begin with Bosola's words to Antonio in Act 3, Scene 5:

> This proclaims your breeding.
> Every small thing draws a base mind to fear,
> As the adamant draws iron; fare you well sir,
> You shall shortly hear from's.

ACTIVITY 12

Do you agree with Bosola's judgement of Antonio?

4 Bosola

'Bosola is no mechanical villain; instead he is a misfit, a man of rather worthier talents forced into a degrading position, and with a brutal philosophy, making the most of it by the thoroughness with which he plays his part.' Do you agree with this assessment of Bosola? Find evidence in the play to support your view of him.

You have already considered Bosola's need for money. Now you could look at his speech after the death of the Duchess in Act 4, Scene 2:

> My estate is sunk
> Below the degree of fear: where were
> These penitent fountains while she was living?
> O, they were frozen up! Here is a sight
> As direful to my soul as is the sword
> Unto a wretch hath slain his father. Come,
> I'll bear thee hence:
> And execute thy last will; that's deliver
> Thy body to the reverent dispose
> Of some good women: that the cruel tyrant
> Shall not deny me. Then I'll post to Milan
> Where somewhat I will speedily enact
> Worth my dejection.

ACTIVITY 13

Do you agree with critics who claim that the most important change in Bosola is the growth of his pity and admiration for the Duchess?

5 Is there any light in the darkness of the play?

It has been claimed that 'if you look into the deepest darkness of the play, there is a flash of light'. Do you agree with this optimistic view of *The Duchess of Malfi?*

You could begin by looking at two areas of the play which might give some hope to the audience. One is Bosola's 'conversion' into a bringer of goodness and destroyer of the evil brothers and their court, referred to in question 4 above. It may also be helpful to consider the Duchess herself as a source of light in the play, for example in her playfulness in the wooing of Antonio in Act 1, Scene 1.

However, her death scene (Act 4, Scene 2) is the scene which most critics would point to as evidence of her strength and majesty: 'I am Duchess of Malfi still [. . .]'.

ACTIVITY 14

1 What opinion do you form of the Duchess here and in the scene as a whole?

2 How do her words and actions reflect upon her brothers?

6 Webster presents his characters with pity – or contempt?

It has been suggested that 'Webster has a kind of pity for all of his characters, an attitude towards good and bad alike . . .'. Do you agree with the interpretation – or does Webster treat some characters with contempt?

You could start by looking at the Cardinal, possibly one of the most evil characters. Webster describes the Cardinal's fear and confusion in Act 5, Scene 5:

When I look into the fish-ponds, in my garden,
Methinks I see a thing, arm'd with a rake
That seems to strike at me: [. . .]

ACTIVITY 15

1 What has happened to the usually confident Cardinal here? What has he seen?

2 Do you think Webster could be playing on the audience's pity in his presentation of the old man's confusion here?

Having explored the six critical perspectives here, you can now use this framework to explore other aspects of the play.

Volpone by Ben Jonson

Volpone belongs partly to the genre of the comedy of humours. People used to believe that there were four 'humours' or liquids in the human body which made a person cheerful, calm, bad-tempered or very melancholy. Ideally, there should be a balance between all of the humours. Jonson modernised this medieval idea, and portrayed his characters with one dominant characteristic; in *Volpone* this is avarice (greed). To focus attention on this vice, he created two-dimensional **caricatures** embodying avarice, but added a little twist of individuality to each. His aim, he declared, was to teach his audience about the inevitable punishment for evil by making them laugh.

The six different critical perspectives on *Volpone* to be discussed here are:

1 Whether the characters are aware of the price they will pay for riches.

2 Whether Jonson's use of caricature is a weakness or a strength.

3 The dramatic relationships between the characters.

4 How far justice is achieved at the end of the play.

5 Whether the play is an exposure of human weakness.

6 How effective Celia is as a stage character.

1 The price for gold

A critic has commented: 'The blasphemous possibilities of magnificence radiate through the play, at tension with the realisation that gold is no more than metal.' Do you think this is a fair analysis of *Volpone*?

Start by trying to paraphrase the quotation. What the critic is saying is that most of the characters in the play seem to want wealth and all the luxury and splendour that goes with it; they are greedy and avaricious. But the audience, unlike most of the characters in the play, will probably know that gold is just a symbol of greed, and that their avarice will be punished.

Next, look at Volpone's attitude to gold, and also Mosca's. Volpone's view is made clear at the beginning of the play (Act 1, Scene 1):

> [. . .] let me kiss,
> With adoration, thee, and every relic
> Of sacred treasure in this blessed room.

ACTIVITY 1

1 What would you say is Volpone's attitude to his gold?

2 Why does Jonson make Volpone address the gold directly?

3 Pick out the words in this speech which relate to religion, and those about wealth. Does the use of the two **registers** suggest that Volpone's attitude is blasphemous?

In his seduction speeches to Celia, for example in Act 3, Scene 2, Volpone stresses the magnificence of his possessions:

> See, a carbuncle
> May put out both the eyes of our St Mark;
> A diamond would have bought Lollia Paulina
> When she came in like star-light, hid with jewels
> That were the spoils of provinces.

ACTIVITY 2

1 How is the sense of magnificence conveyed in these words?

2 In the reference to Lollia Paulina, how are the jewels put to use?

3 Is there some ambiguity in the reference to St Mark?

4 Why does Jonson refer to the 'spoils of provinces'?

Mosca is also made to share this obsession with gold and wealth. For example, talking to Voltore after the first trial (Act 4, Scene 2), he says:

> I'd have your tongue, sir, tipped with gold for this.

ACTIVITY 3

1 What do these lines reveal about Mosca's values?

2 Why does Mosca use the comparison of Celia with gold to impress Volpone (at Act 1, Scene 1)?

3 Is there any irony in using such a comparison with Celia?

To develop your answer, you could also examine some of the other characters in the play. Are there any exceptions to those in pursuit of wealth? Could such characters represent the moral viewpoint, or the view of the audience? Finally, you would need to respond with your own opinion about the critic's view.

2 Is the use of caricature a weakness or a strength?

Some critics claim that in *Volpone* 'the aim of a great realist for truth and nature never overcame the satirist's and humorist's weakness for fantastic caricature'. Another critic takes a different view, saying that *Volpone* 'is an art of caricature, of great caricature'. Which opinion do you find more acceptable?

First consider both views, and then draw your own conclusion.

The use of caricature is a weakness

You could begin by summarising Jonson's use of caricature in the play. There are the five central characters: Volpone the fox; Voltore the vulture; Mosca the fly; Corbaccio the raven; and Corvino the crow.

ACTIVITY 4

1 What do their names tell you about their characters?

2 Which qualities of a fox does Volpone possess?

3 Why is Mosca later called a 'flesh-fly'?

4 What is Voltore ravenous for?

5 The raven and the crow are birds of carrion. What is the 'carrion' that they are preying on?

You could expand this answer by pointing out that in *Volpone* there is a wide range of character types. For example, Sir Politic Would-be, whom Peregrine describes in Act 2, Scene 1:

> O, this knight,
> Were he well known, would be a precious thing
> To fit our English stage: [. . .]

ACTIVITY 5

1 To what extent do you agree with Peregrine's judgement here?

2 Is Sir Politic Would-be anything more than a fool? Is he evil?

3 What is his dramatic purpose in the play on stage?

Peregrine also comments on Lady Would-be (Act 2, Scene 1), who:

> Lies here in Venice, for intelligence
> Of tires and fashions, and behaviour,
> Among the courtesans? the fine Lady Would-be?

ACTIVITY 6

1 What is Peregrine's opinion of Lady Would-be?

2 What do you think her interests are?

3 Taking Lady Would-be in the context of the whole play, is she evil or foolish? What is she used to satirise?

4 Do you think that she is just a caricature, or does she have more rounded dramatic qualities?

Celia and Bonario can perhaps be seen as different character types from the others, for example when the first Avocator asks (Act 4, Scene 2):

> What witnesses have you
> To make good your report?
>
> BONARIO   Our consciences.
>
> CELIA   And heaven, that never fails the innocent.

ACTIVITY 7

1 Why does Jonson make the reference to heaven here?

2 What effect is created by making Celia's words run on from those of Bonario?

3 What might Celia and Bonario represent in the play? Are they simply caricatures?

The use of caricature is a strength

Having investigated the range of character types in the play, you should then focus on the second view that Volpone is 'great caricature'. You could approach this by showing how Jonson develops the caricatures. Look at Volpone's words at the trial (Act 5, Scene 1):

> I shall have instantly my vulture, crow,
> Raven come flying hither, on the news,
> To peck for carrion, my she-wolf and all,
> Greedy and full of expectation –

ACTIVITY 8

1 What do these words tell you about Volpone's attitude to the other characters and to himself?

2 Does Volpone have a dramatic function as a commentator and also as a participant?

3 Does this suggest that Volpone, with some self-awareness, is more than just a two-dimensional caricature?

Corvino can also be seen to be treated ironically. He attacks Celia for talking with the disguised Volpone (Act 2, Scene 3):

Death of mine honour, with the city's fool,
A juggling, tooth-drawing, prating mountebank?

But literally minutes later, perhaps overcome by avarice, he plots with Mosca to allow Volpone to seduce his wife. The playwright then takes this change-of-heart one step further, when Corvino begs Mosca:

[. . .] swear it was
On the first hearing, as thou mayst do truly –
Mine own free motion.

ACTIVITY 9

1 Does the audience still see Corvino as a simple stereotype after witnessing this scene?

2 Do you find Jonson's use of irony amusing?

3 What is the overall effect of this scene on your attitude to Corvino? And to Celia?

Mosca is also treated in a similarly ironical way. After the first trial, Mosca and Volpone seem delighted and satisfied (Act 5, Scene 1):

MOSCA   [. . .] We must here be fixed;
           Here we must rest; this is our masterpiece:
           We cannot think to go beyond this.

VOLPONE   True, [. . .]

ACTIVITY 10

1 What decision have Mosca and Volpone reached? Do they stick to it?

2 What will be the effect of taking their scheming further?

3 Why does Jonson split the final line here between Mosca and Volpone?

4 What is implied by the word 'masterpiece'?

5 Do you think this scene contributes to the idea of a two-dimensional stereotype?

To complete your answer you now need to add your own opinion about Jonson's art of caricature, for instance you could discuss whether Jonson presents realistic social problems in non-realistic ways.

3 The relationships between the characters

'If change does not occur in the inner life of Jonson's characters, it occurs constantly in the relationships they bear to each other.' Does this comment apply to the relationship between characters in *Volpone*?

In Activity 8 you looked at one of the exchanges between Corvino and Mosca. Now look at the relationship between Mosca and Volpone at the second trial when they have a quick exchange in Act 5, Scene 7:

> MOSCA [*aside*]   Will you give me half?
>
> VOLPONE [*aside*] First I'll be hanged.
>
> MOSCA [*aside*]   I know
>   Your voice is good, cry not so loud.

ACTIVITY 11

1 What change has occurred in the relationship between Volpone and Mosca?

2 How significant are these lines coming at the ending of the play?

3 Why do you think Jonson uses 'asides' here and elsewhere in the play?

4 How far is justice achieved at the end of the play?

Ben Jonson wrote: 'It is the office of a comick-poet to imitate justice.' Do you think that he achieves this aim in *Volpone*? How far does the play go in fulfilling this?

You could begin by looking at the sort of punishments offered at the end of the play to Mosca, Volpone, Corbaccio and Corvino.

ACTIVITY 12

1 Do you think that the punishments are just? Or, as some critics think, are they too savage for the ending of a comedy?

2 Could there be another interpretation of 'justice' in this play? Is it just to ridicule these men, when all of society itself seems to be rotten?

5 Does the play expose human weakness?

The play has been described as 'a lacerating exposure of human weaknesses, and a searching criticism of the society of its day'. How far do you agree with this assessment of *Volpone*?

You have already looked at evidence from the play to help you answer this question. It might be helpful now to start with Jonson's words in the Prologue:

> Whose true scope, if you would know it,
> In all his poems still hath been this measure,
>   To mix profit with your pleasure; [. . .]

ACTIVITY 13

1 What might the 'pleasure' be for an audience attending this play?

2 What might the 'profit' be?

6 How effective is Celia as a stage character?

Several critics believe that Celia represents Christian virtue in the play. But it is also argued that her speeches are 'desperately wooden', and that 'she remains an unknown character in the play'. Bearing these two assessments in mind, what is your response to Celia?

You could start by looking at the seduction scene. Many critics think that Celia is colourless and lifeless, but perhaps there is more to her than this. Look, for example, at Act 3, Scene 2, where Volpone talks of dressing Celia up:

> Then will I have thee in more modern forms,
> Attired like some spritely dame of France,
> Brave Tuscan lady, or proud Spanish beauty;
> Sometimes unto the Persian Sophy's wife;
> Or the Grand Signor's mistress; and for change,
> To one of our most artful courtesans,
> Or some quick Negro, or cold Russian;
> And I will meet thee in as many shapes,
> Where we may, so, transfuse our wandering souls
> Out at our lips, and score up sums of pleasures, [. . .]

Celia responds simply and without bluster: 'If you have touch of holy saints [. . .]'.

ACTIVITY 14

1 Do you think that Celia's plain and simple language can be made effective on stage?

2 Can Celia be seen to represent virtue in a diseased and fickle world?

Now you have examined the six critical perspectives here, continue to use the model framework to explore other aspects of the play.

Assessment Objective 5ii

The dominant Assessment Objective in this section of Module 4 is AO5ii.

Candidates will be expected to:

> evaluate the significance of cultural, historical and other contextual influences on literary texts and study.

At A2 Level, four types of context are specified:

- the context of period or era including significant social, historical, political and cultural processes

- the context of the work in terms of the writer's biography or milieu

- the language context, including relevant episodes in the use and development of literary language, the question of **demotic**, colloquial or dialect styles

- the different contexts established by the work's reception over time, including the recognition that texts have different meanings and effects in different period.

This module also tests – to a lesser extent – Assessment Objectives 1, 2 and 3. These objectives should be covered as you discuss ideas relating to the context.

Romanticism

All of the poets represented in this section of Module 4 are known as 'Romantic' poets. Romantic poets reacted against many aspects of eighteenth-century thought, including

- Rationalism – the belief that the world is controlled by reason. Instead, the Romantic poets rejected certain ideas about the importance of reason, emphasising instead the importance of the imagination. Visions of society as a sort of machine, within which individuals have an allotted function, were also rejected

- Classicism – the Romantics hated the well-structured formal language of eighteenth-century poetry. They preferred loose forms, expressing personal feelings

- organised religion – the Romantic poets were not necessarily anti-religious, but their religion was far more personal and subjective. Their view of religion was often not orthodox, at times revering God-in-nature, or the **pantheism** of the ancient Greeks.

To counteract these earlier ideas, Wordsworth and Coleridge first defined their ideas in the *Lyrical Ballads* of 1798. The power of the imagination over reason was stressed; Nature was to be seen as evidence of a living God (the doctrine of pantheism); experience was to be gained through the senses rather than reason; and language used was to be the everyday language of man.

But there was no collective sense about the Romantic movement. Each of the poets you will study here is an individual, sharing some, but not all of the characteristics of Romanticism and some, but not all of the ideas of the other writers labelled as Romantics. You will see that these poets sought what they believed were more appropriate ways of expressing these 'modern' attitudes.

At A2 Level you are required to explore the context as well as the text, although this does not mean that you should spend excessive time studying context. However, it is essential that you understand the links between the context and the text in the ideas and manner of expression of the writers. In this way you will 'evaluate the significance of the context'.

Example of a context

The French Revolution provided a historical and a political context, for example, for some of the poems of Blake, and for Helen Maria Williams, who lived in Paris during the Revolution. You should be aware that the experience of the French Revolution affected the ideas and expressions of the poetry but you do not need to know all the details of the Revolution itself. What you need to do is show awareness of how the poets' reactions to this event coloured their thoughts – what it was about the Revolution that sparked off particular responses, and how this context affected the poets' ideas and writing.

Finally, since all the poets in this section are Romantic poets, each time you write about the poetry you will be addressing the literary context, exploring some aspect of it, as well as any other particular context you may be investigating.

Method of exploring contexts

The method will be similar to that used in Section A on drama. For each poem four contexts will be selected and illustrated in a sample response for you to develop in your own time. Another two contexts will be suggested for further exercises, with a starting point for you to build an answer on. You will look at how the context is apparent in the ideas of the poetry, and also how these ideas are expressed, because the method of expression is itself part of the Romantic literary context. The word 'primary' is used to describe the particular context explored in each of the sub-sections because, as you will see, there are almost always overlaps between contexts.

Women Romantic Poets

Six primary contexts will be looked at here:

1 The political context – Helen Maria Williams.

2 The context of nature – Dorothy Wordsworth.

3 Social and literary contexts – Elizabeth Hands.

4 Contexts of childhood and society – Mary Lamb.

5 Social contexts and the situation of women – Carolina Nairne.

6 The social, cultural and historical context of women in society – Joanna Baillie.

1 The political context

To begin considering this context, look at Helen Maria Williams's response to the French Revolution. To evaluate the context, you may assess how the French Revolution has influenced her poetry. You can see this in these lines from her poem 'To Dr Moore, In Answer to a Poetical Epistle Written by Him in Wales' (lines 37–40):

> For now on Gallia's plains the peasant knows
> Those equal rights impartial heaven bestows.
> He now, by freedom's ray illumined, taught
> Some self-respect, some energy of thought, [. . .]

ACTIVITY 1

1 Why does the poet make the reference to Gallia? And to the peasants?

2 What was the slogan of the French Revolution?

3 Is this slogan referred to here and elsewhere in the poem?

4 Why does the poet use the words 'heaven bestows?' What might these words suggest about her attitude to the French Revolution? Do you think that she approves of it?

Helen Williams goes on to consider 'reason', one of the bugbears of the Romantic poets (lines 49–50):

> Those reasoners who pretend that each abuse,
> Sanctioned by precedent, has some blest use!

5 Why does the poet think the abuses in society have been allowed to continue?

6 Could reason be seen as the basis for the traditional powers of kings and other powerful authorities?

7 Does the poet think that reason has been used to take advantage of certain people in society?

8 Does she approve of the outcome of the Revolution in sweeping this sort of destructive reason away?

ACTIVITY 2

How the presentation develops this context:

1 How would you describe the tone of the whole poem? Does it teach a lesson? (This is known as **didactic** poetry.)

2 How does this philosophy relate to the ideas of Romanticism?

3 Is the register formal or informal? Why do you think this is?

4 What is the purpose of religious references such as 'heaven' and 'blest'?

You should now be able to make an evaluation of the significance of the political context in this poem. You could also ask yourself such questions as:

• What was the contextual frame which influenced the poet's ideas in this poem?

• How has this political event influenced the poet's attitudes and style?

You should also appreciate that the political context overlaps with several other contexts:

• social, since it affected the people within the society of France

• historical, since it was one of the major events of the eighteenth century

• cultural, since the Revolution indicated a swing in cultural attitudes

• biographical, as the poet lived in France and witnessed events.

In the attack on suppressed 'Liberty' you could also discuss, for example, Hannah More's poem 'Slavery'.

2 The context of nature

This context may be explored in Dorothy Wordsworth's poem 'Floating Island'. This island was at Hawkshead on Lake Windermere in the Lake District, where Dorothy lived with her brother William. She shared his views about the value of nature as a teacher, and as a link with God. The poet explains how the island was 'loosed from its hold' (lines 11–16):

Float, with its crest of trees adorned
On which the warbling birds their pastime take.

Food, shelter, safety there they find
There berries ripen, flowerets bloom;
There insects live their lives – and die:
A peopled *world* it is; in size a tiny room.

ACTIVITY 3

1 What aspects of nature are seen on the island?

2 What does the poet tell you about the inhabitants?

3 Is there a sense of harmony or of disharmony?

ACTIVITY 4

How the presentation develops this context:

1 Why are words such as 'adorned', 'take', 'food', 'ripen' and 'bloom' used?

2 Why does the poet use so many nouns, such as 'Food', 'shelter', 'safety'?

3 What effect does the word 'warbling' have?

4 What does the poet compare the island to?

The context of nature overlaps here with the philosophical context of the Romantic poet. To evaluate these you might ask yourself such questions as:

ACTIVITY 5

1 How does Dorothy Wordsworth regard nature?

2 Does she gain insight into human life from her study of nature? Could this be why she refers to the 'world' and a 'room'?

3 Why do you think the poet refers to the fact that insects 'die'? Does she express grief over this, or does she accept it?

4 How does this poem fit with the Romantic vision, in the way that nature can be a teacher to man?

You could compare this poem with Joanna Baillie's 'A Summer's Day', for example.

3 Social and literary contexts

Elizabeth Hands was a servant by profession – this was her social, economic and biographical context. She wrote poetry about social attitudes and social pretensions. These two contexts are intertwined in her poem. 'A Poem, on the Supposition of an Advertisement Appearing in a Morning Paper, of the Publication of a Volume of Poems, by a Servant-Maid'. In these lines from the poem (lines 11 ff.) she anticipates the reactions of society ladies to her poetry:

'A servant write verses!' says Madam Du Bloom:
'Pray what is the subject – a mop, or a broom?' [. . .]
Had she wrote a receipt, to've instructed you how
To warm a cold breast of veal, like a ragout,
Or to make cowslip wine, that would pass for champagne,
It might have been useful, again and again.'

ACTIVITY 6

The social context:

1 What do these lines reveal about the class structure of the period?

2 What are the attitudes here and in the poem as a whole of the wealthy to their employees?

3 Does the servant have support for her efforts from any of the ladies?

4 What is the speaker's attitudes to her employers?

5 What do the names of the ladies suggest? What are their interests?

ACTIVITY 7

Looking at the way the poet also draws in the literary context:

1 Why do you think that the title of the poem is so long?

2 How would you define the register of the poem?

3 Why does the poet use dialogue? What effect does this create?

4 What do the domestic references imply about the role of women in that society?

5 What is the effect of the use of **heroic rhyming couplets**?

6 Do you consider the poem to be a **satire** on society and social attitudes?

Within the literary context you might find it useful to compare the tea ceremony and the card game with Pope's account of these in *The Rape of The Lock*, Canto 111. Pope used this form to satirise society. Does Hands also?

• Do you think there are any serious 'messages' behind the mocking facade?

You could also link this poem with Anne Grant's 'A Familiar Epistle to a Friend'.

4 Contexts of childhood and society

Mary Lamb experienced poverty as a child, and wrote about this subject from personal experience. In her poem 'Choosing a Profession', she tells of a young Creole child brought from the West Indies to be educated in England. The speaker realises that he is not accepted at the Preparatory School (lines 5–6):

When from his artless tale the mistress found
The child had not one friend on English ground, [. . .]

The lady waits for the child to decide what he wants to do in his future life (lines 17–21):

Till on a day at length he to her came,
Joy sparkling in his eyes; and said, the same
Trade he would be those boys of colour were,
Who danced so happy in the open air.
It was a troop of chimney-sweeping boys, [. . .]

ACTIVITY 8

The social context of childhood:

1 What view of childhood does Mary Lamb convey here?

2 In the poem as a whole, how is the boy treated in the posh English school?

3 Why does the boy identify with the chimney-sweepers?

4 What is the 'mistress's' attitude to the boy? Is it typical?

5 Is there a sense of cruelty to any particular groups of children here and in the poem as a whole?

6 Is the title of the poem ironic?

ACTIVITY 9

How the language develops this context:

1 How would you describe the overall tone of the poem?

2 What is the effect of the poet's use of a jaunty four-stressed line?

3 Look at the language related to the children and their activities: 'wooden music', 'tarnish'd finery', 'grotesque array'. What sort of spectacle do the children create? Is it 'normal' social behaviour?

4 Why do you think that the children's music is described as 'wooden'?

5 From your knowledge of the lives of the chimney-sweepers of this period, do you think that they are really dancing because they are happy?

You can see that the context has been widened to include criticism of the society which creates injustices towards children. To clarify how this might be achieved, ask yourself some further questions:

ACTIVITY 10

1 How does Mary Lamb convey the innocence of the Creole child? And of the chimney-sweepers?

2 Look closely at the discrepancy between the attitude of the children in the poem, and yours as a reader. Could this be used to highlight the exploitation of children disadvantaged by colour or class, and the experience of the reader who knows the horrors they really face?

3 Think about how this discrepancy is at the root of Mary Lamb's method of creating irony. How does she use it to criticise the society which acts so cruelly?

In responding to all these questions, you will have evaluated the significance of the social and moral context.

This poem could also be compared with Jane Taylor's poem 'Poverty'.

5 Social contexts and the situation of women

You could explore this context by looking at Carolina Oliphant Nairne's poem 'The Laird o'Cockpen', beginning with the last two verses. You may begin your enquiry by asking yourself some questions:

ACTIVITY 11

1 What is the significance of the title? Is it serious or comic?

2 What is the man's attitude to the woman regarding love or sex?

3 How does the woman respond to him?

4 What does the poem suggest about the rights of men and women as far as sex is concerned? Do you think that there is any equality?

You could link this with Anna Dodsworth's poem 'To Matthew Dodsworth, Esq.'.

You could also explore the language context in 'The Laird o'Cockpen', and consider why the poet writes in a Scottish dialect. What effect does she want to achieve?

6 The social, cultural and historical context of women in society

To explore this context, consider Joanna Baillie's poem 'A Mother to Her Waking Infant', beginning with the last stanza.

ACTIVITY 12

1 How does the mother feel towards her child?

2 How does the language throughout the poem suggest her attitude?

3 How is the social isolation of the mother suggested?

4 Look at the last line of the poem: 'Thou dost not heed my lay.' Could these words be addressed to more people than just the baby?

5 What is the poet saying about women and domesticity and motherhood in this period? What are the social options for a woman as an individual or a poet in this period?

You could also discuss Anna Barbauld's 'The Rights of Women' here. In focusing on women's rights you have will also evaluated the significance of the social, cultural and historical contexts.

Using this model framework, carry on to explore other contents related to these poems on your own.

The Prelude (1805) *Book First* and *Book Second* by William Wordsworth

To many readers, William Wordsworth defined and embodied in his writings the concepts behind Romantic poetry. *The Prelude* is generally regarded as an important statement about the ideals and purposes, and also of the methods of writing Romantic poetry. Wordsworth explores his relationship with nature and the crucial role it has played over the years in his development as a poet.

The six primary contexts here are:

1 The biographical context.

2 The literary, historical and cultural contexts.

3 The context of nature.

4 The language context.

5 The philosophical context.

6 The religious context.

The biographical context

This is an important context in the study of *The Prelude*. Since the poem is written as a first-person account of the poet's own experiences, it is autobiographical.

In considering how Wordsworth shapes his autobiographical poem you will look at the use of first-person narrative; the handling of time; flashes of memory; the metaphor of a journey; and moments of revelation.

The use of first-person narrative

The first-person account determines the shape and the structure of *The Prelude*, as in the following example (*Book First*, 59–63):

> [. . .] To the open fields I told
> A prophesy; poetic numbers came
> Spontaneously, and clothed in priestly robe
> My spirit, thus singled out, as it might seem,
> For holy services. Great hopes were mine: [. . .]

ACTIVITY 1

1 *Book First* is sub-titled 'Introduction: Childhood and School-time'. How old was Wordsworth when he wrote *The Prelude*?

2 Does he write about his thoughts and activities as they occur?

3 What is he looking for as he writes? Or has he achieved all his goals?

4 Would you say that the account of his search helps to shape the structure of the autobiographical account?

The handling of time

Wordsworth makes the purpose of the poem clear from the beginning of *Book First* (lines 29–32):

> [. . .] Whither shall I turn,
> By road or pathway, or through open field,
> Or shall a twig or any floating thing
> Upon the river point me out my course?

ACTIVITY 2

1 What question is Wordsworth really asking himself here?

2 Why does Wordsworth use the present tense here?

3 Does this question lead you to expect a straightforward chronological account of Wordsworth's search?

4 Given that these words are spoken by the mature poet, what has actually happened to the chronological sequence? And is this how the past is recalled – through odd moments or in isolated events, rather than as a straightforward sequence of time?

Wordsworth's flashes of memory

Wordsworth punctuates his autobiographical account with flashes of memory of particular moments or events. For example, the flashes seem to be occasions and events taken from his younger life, like the 'boating' episode (*Book First*, 372–5):

> One evening – surely I was led by her –
> I went alone into a shepherd's boat,
> A skiff that to a willow-tree was tied
> Within a rocky cove, its usual home.

ACTIVITY 3

1 How does the poet's use of language help convey the 'reality' of the situation?

2 It might help to make a list of the 'realistic' events which occur in *Book First* and *Book Second*. What is their purpose, compared to the philosophical contemplations within the poem?

3 Do the 'realistic' events help to chart the progress of the poet as he grows up? Does each episode have special significance in his development?

The metaphor of a journey

It has been suggested that the whole of *The Prelude* is an account of Wordsworth's journey through time, place and thought, punctuated by flashes of memory. This is clear at the very beginning of the poem (*Book First*, 11–13):

> What dwelling shall receive me, in what vale
> Shall be my harbour, underneath what grove
> Shall I take up my home [. . .]?

The journey **motif** is one that Wordsworth refers to frequently, as in *Book First*, lines 110 ff.

ACTIVITY 4

1 How does Wordsworth suggest the idea of a journey here?

2 Why do you think Wordsworth uses a question in the quotation above?

3 Why do you think that he keeps referring back to the 'journey' image? Think about how this might relate to the structure of, and the purposes behind, *The Prelude*. What do you think these purposes are?

Moments of revelation

Wordsworth does not allow the reader to forget about his quest, as in these lines (*Book Second*, 321 ff.):

[. . .] For I would walk alone
In storm and tempest, [. . .] and I would stand
Beneath some rock, listening to sounds that are
The ghostly language of the ancient earth, [. . .]
Thence did I drink the visionary power.

ACTIVITY 5

1 What is Wordsworth describing in these lines?

2 Look at the tense he is using. What effect does this have?

3 Why do you think Wordsworth keeps reminding the reader of these moments? Do they help you to understand the poet? If so, how?

2 The literary, historical and cultural contexts

These contexts are central to an awareness of how Wordsworth has come to terms with himself as a poet – the **archetype** of a Romantic poet. There are four areas that can be explored here: the memory of things past; Wordsworth's idea of the senses; the joining together of his own internal worlds with the external world represented by nature; the role of the poet.

The memory of things past

Wordsworth makes very clear the importance of recalling the past; he talks of being endowed with 'high objects' and 'enduring things' which:

[. . .] purifying thus
The elements of feeling and of thought,
And sanctifying by such discipline
Both pain and fear, until we recognise
A grandeur in the beatings of the heart.

(*The Prelude Book First*, 47–51)

ACTIVITY 6

1 What is Wordsworth saying here about his thought processes?

2 Is there a link here to his notion of 'emotions recollected in tranquillity'?

3 Do you think *The Prelude* consists of emotions recollected in tranquillity?

Wordsworth's ideas of the senses

Wordsworth talks about sense and sensations in *The Prelude* in his account of the 'infant babe' (*Book Second*, 252 ff.):

His organs and recipient faculties
Are quickened [. . .]
And those sensations which have been derived
From this beloved presence – there exists
A virtue which irradiates and exalts
All objects through all intercourse of sense.

ACTIVITY 7

1 How important are 'sense' and 'sensations' to Wordsworth's idea of a poet?

2 How might the word 'sensations' be interpreted here and in the poem as a whole? Think about the sensations felt by the baby from his mother, and the **sensuous** response of the poet to the beauty of nature.

3 Does Wordsworth analyse how the senses bring about the sensations which he feels?

4 Does he suggest that sensations are more important than reason?

The joining together of Wordsworth's internal world with the external world represented by nature

Wordsworth refers to this joining together, or **fusion**, during the course of the poem, when he thinks of past experiences, for example in *Book Second*, lines 28–36:

[. . .] so wide appears
The vacancy between me and those days,
Which yet have such self-presence in my mind
That sometimes when I think of them I seem
Two consciousnesses – conscious of myself,
And of some other being. A grey stone
Of native rock, left midway in the square
Of our small market-village, was the home
And centre of these joys; [. . .]

ACTIVITY 8

1 How many types of 'fusions' can you find in these lines? Think first about the internal fusion or joining together of the poet in the past with the present. What does the 'vacancy' he refers to suggest?

2 Now think about the other 'fusion', that of the 'two consciousnesses'.

   • What might the first 'consciousness' be?

   • For the second 'consciousness' think about what the 'grey stone' of nature conveys to the poet.

3 Could there be two sorts of fusions indicated in these lines?

The role of the poet

At the beginning of the poem, Wordsworth writes 'Whither shall I turn [. . .]?' (*Book First*, 29). Of course, as a reader you know exactly where he has turned to because *The Prelude* is an account of self-discovery, an imaginative journey. Wordsworth expresses clearly how he sees the role of the poet (*Book First*, 61–3) as you saw on page 59:

[. . .] and clothed in priestly robe
My spirit, thus singled out, as it might seem,
For holy services. [. . .]

ACTIVITY 9

1 How does Wordsworth describe the role of the poet?

2 Why does he use language related to religious services?

3 Does he see this role as important for teaching his fellow man?

3 The context of nature

There are three areas to be considered: the powerful effect of nature on the poet; what the poet sees in nature; the idea of the **sublime** in Wordsworth's poetry.

The powerful effect of nature on the poet

Wordsworth often expresses his debt to nature, for example, in *Book First*, lines 490–4:

> Ye presences of Nature, in the sky
> Or on the earth, ye visions of the hills
> And souls of lonely places, can I think
> A vulgar hope was yours when ye employed
> Such ministry [. . .]?

ACTIVITY 10

1 How does Wordsworth acknowledge his debt to nature here?

2 What sort of language and register does he use? Why?

3 How does he see his relationship with nature?

What the poet sees in nature

Wordsworth explores at length the relationship between nature and his response as a poet. The image of the babe which was discussed in Activity 7 seems to clarify his ideas about this (*Book Second*, 269–76):

> For feeling has to him imparted strength,
> And – powerful in all sentiments of grief,
> Of exultation, fear and joy – his mind,
> Even as an agent of the one great mind,
> Creates, creator and receiver both,
> Working but in alliance with the works
> Which it beholds. – Such, verily, is the first
> Poetic spirit of our human life; [. . .]

ACTIVITY 11

1 How does Wordsworth describe the relationship between poet and nature here?

2 How is the double role of the poet explained as 'creator and receiver'?

3 Does Wordsworth see nature as proof of the divine? Does he see a harmonious link between the **natural universe** and the divine universe, God and man working together?

4 When you read the descriptions of nature in *The Prelude* what effect do these words have on you? Can you look beyond the actual description to understand the lesson Wordsworth is trying to teach?

The idea of the 'sublime' in Wordsworth's poetry

Wordsworth uses this word to describe his pleasure in the beauty of nature. For him, this beauty suggests something divine (*Book Second*, 318–21):

> [. . .] difference
> Perceived in things where to the common eye
> No difference is, and hence, from the same source,
> Sublimer joy.

ACTIVITY 12

1 How do you think Wordsworth's perception of nature differs from that of an ordinary person?

2 By what means has he discovered these differences?

3 What are the implications of the word 'sublime'? Does the poet see God through nature? Is this intense kind of emotional and spiritual experience opposed to a belief in the power of reason?

4 The language context

Throughout *The Prelude* Wordsworth employs certain recurrent sequences of images which include: water, a boat, an island, and solitariness.

Water

There is an example of this imagery when Wordsworth rows the stolen skiff and describes the patterns on the water in *Book First*, lines 391–4:

> Leaving behind her still on either side
> Small circles glittering idly in the moon,
> Until they melted all into one track
> Of sparking light.

ACTIVITY 13

1 Do you think the water the poet describes here is physically real?

2 What other associations does the water have? Think about the 'unreal' world of contemplation; the water as a symbol of transition for the reader, from the observation of natural life to inner contemplation.

3 Do you think the water works as an image which draws together the themes of *The Prelude*?

The boat

The same lines quoted above suggest that the boat image works in a similar way to the water imagery.

ACTIVITY 14

1 Do the same comments apply to the boat as to the water in Activity 13?

2 Think about the boat as a symbol of the transportation of the poet from the 'real' world to the world of contemplation.

The island and solitariness

You could combine a discussion of the image of the island with that of solitariness. Look at Wordsworth's description of the boys rowing around Windermere from *Book Second*, lines 63–7:

And now a third small island where remained
An old stone table, and a mouldered cave,
A hermit's history. In such a race,
So ended, disappointment could be none,
Uneasiness, or pain, or jealousy: [. . .]

ACTIVITY 15

1 What effect has the sight of the island had on Wordsworth?

2 Does it matter any more who wins the race?

3 What does Wordsworth suggest about the quality of life here? Does it seem attractive?

4 Can you see a similar transition from the 'real' to the contemplative as in *Book First*, lines 391–4 above?

5 Why is solitariness important here?

6 Try to work out how the vision of the island is related to Wordsworth's flashes of memory, discussed on page 60 above.

The exploration of the language context (AO3) overlaps here with Assessment Objective 5ii. Wordsworth was responsible for incorporating these types of images into the standard register of Romantic poetry. By assessing these images you are exploring one aspect of the change in language in the poetry of the period. To expand this discussion you could look at Wordsworth's use of 'everyday' language in a formal poem, such as 'It was a splendid evening'.

5 The philosophical context

To explore this context, you could consider the attitude to, and the way of life which Wordsworth advocates in *The Prelude*. Look in particular at the passage in *Book Second*, lines 217–20, which begins 'Science appears but what in truth she is [. . .]'.

ACTIVITY 16

What is Wordsworth implying here? What does he recommend instead?

6 The religious context

Wordsworth evidently saw nature as evidence of the divine. You could explore this context by looking at the passage beginning 'If this be error, . . .' in *Book Second*, lines 435–46.

ACTIVITY 17

1 What do you think is the basis of Wordsworth's religion?

2 How are these beliefs revealed elsewhere in *The Prelude*?

Using this model framework, you can now go on to explore other contexts related to *The Prelude*.

Songs of Innocence and *Songs of Experience* by William Blake

In his poetry, William Blake explores the relationship between individuals and society. In his *Songs of Innocence* there are harmonious relationships between human beings, and between humans and God, resulting in a mutual trust and happiness in an open society. But Blake is honest about the times in which he lived. He saw, for example, the hopes for the French Revolution crushed by the first Terrors of 1792. He witnessed poverty and exploitation in London, and the oppression caused by the Industrial Revolution. In a radical way, he reworked the **pastoral** conventions from the first songs to create his *Songs of Experience*. In these poems, he asks how man can survive in a grimly oppressive society. He suggests that the answer might be by learning some sort of wisdom from experience. The irony, of course, is that this wisdom, like the Fall from Eden, must be bought at the cost of a certain naive innocence. In his poems Blake produces a series of myths in order to explore the 'new' human condition, to replace the 'outworn' myths of the Bible.

The six primary contexts here are:

1 The social context of childhood.

2 The political context.

3 The context of society and human relationships.

4 The **socialist** political context.

5 The psychological context.

6 The philosophical context of Blake as a **visionary** and prophetic Romantic poet.

1 The social context of childhood

Start by considering what Blake uses childhood to symbolise, and how his language develops the contextual ideas. Read the first stanza of 'The Lamb', and then work through the activity questions below:

> Little Lamb who made thee
> Dost thou know who made thee
> Gave thee life & bid thee feed,
> By the stream & o'er the mead;
> Gave thee clothing of delight,
> Softest clothing wooly bright;
> Gave thee such a tender voice,
> Making all the vales rejoice:
> Little Lamb who made thee
> Dost thou know who made thee

ACTIVITY 1

1 What sort of world is Blake writing about here? Are there any similarities to descriptions of the Garden of Eden?

2 Read the second stanza as well, and decide whether the world that Blake is writing about is a universe controlled by a kindly, paternal God.

ACTIVITY 2

How the presentation develops this context:

1 Look at the simplicity of the language. Does it resemble the language of a child?

3 Why does Blake use repetition in this poem?

4 Why do you think there are no question marks although questions are asked? Are these questions answered in the second stanza?

This consideration of Blake's use of language draws out other contexts – the literary and the historical contexts.

ACTIVITY 3

1 In conveying in the poem the imaginative honesty of a child, what do you think Blake is saying about the state of adulthood?

2 Do you think this is an original and authentic way of expressing the language of a child?

3 How do you think the innocence of the child relates to the innocence of man before the Fall from Eden?

4 How does this world compare with the diseased contemporary society implied in *Songs of Experience*? Could man ever go back to the state of earlier innocence?

In exploring these questions you will have evaluated the significance of the context of childhood as a contrasted image to his contemporary society.

2 The political context

After *Songs of Innocence* appeared in 1789, Blake published *The French Revolution* in 1791. He seemed to be both attracted to and horrified by events during the French Revolution, approving of the revolt against the authority of the kings, but appalled by the anarchy the Revolution unleashed. It is generally believed that these attitudes are expressed in 'The Tyger'. Read the first two stanzas of 'The Tyger':

Tyger Tyger, burning bright,
In the forests of the night;
What immortal hand or eye,
Could frame thy fearful symmetry?

In what distant deeps or skies,
Burnt the fire of thine eyes?
On what wings dare he aspire?
What the hand, dare sieze the fire?

ACTIVITY 4

1 What sort of universe is Blake describing here?

2 How does it compare to the universe portrayed in 'The Lamb'? Think about the ways things are described as man-made and machine-made.

3 Now read the whole poem. What overall impression do you get of this world? Is it full of kindness and goodness?

4 Why might the stars 'water heaven with their tears'? Think about the Fall from Eden again and the sinful state of man.

5 Or could Blake be suggesting something more complex? Is the world represented in 'The Lamb' really the ideal? Does man perhaps need to experience the darker world represented by 'The Tyger' as a transitional stage towards a better universe?

ACTIVITY 5

How the presentation develops this context:

1 Look at the register of the language. How would you describe it?

2 Why are all the questions unanswered?

3 What is the purpose of these images of violent creation and terror?

4 Why is the language left grammatically incomplete?

5 What effect does the use of **incantatory** repetition have throughout the poem?

As you can see, other contexts have been drawn in, including the historical and social context of the Industrial Revolution.

ACTIVITY 6

1 What might the maker/forger of the tyger symbolise?

2 How might mechanical creation suggest the idea of the Industrial Revolution?

3 How does Blake view the power of men and machines?

4 Is Blake making a political statement here?

3 The context of society and human relationships

As well as making clear comments on the direction in which society is heading, Blake offers certain insights into the nature of human relationships, as seen in his poem 'The Sick Rose'. These observations are about relationships between people, and between people, their social sphere and their moral and spiritual contexts.

O Rose, thou art sick.
The invisible worm,
That flies in the night
In the howling storm:

Has found out thy bed
Of crimson joy:
And his dark secret love
Does thy life destroy.

Relationships between people

ACTIVITY 7

1 Does the name 'Rose' suggest that the poem might be about a woman?

2 Similarly, what does 'his dark secret love' suggest about male power?

3 Do you think the words 'worm' and 'bed' could have sexual meanings?

4 If so, what kind of sickness could Blake be alluding to? Could this type of love 'destroy' the lovers?

Relationships between people, their social sphere and their moral and spiritual contexts

ACTIVITY 8

1 Taking a different approach, could the Rose be said to represent England?

2 If so, what might the state of 'night' be referring to? Think about the social conditions of the time, the Industrial Revolution, etc.?

3 What then is the implication for society's effect on the individual? Will it help its members or destroy them?

ACTIVITY 9

How the presentation develops this context:

Explore the series of images which Blake uses in this poem:

- the rose, an image from gardens and a symbol of England

- the worm, also associated with gardens; but in addition the old word for a dragon

- the worm could be the serpent of Eden, as Blake again echoes the religious 'myth' of the Fall of Adam and Eve

- 'bed' and 'crimson' may suggest sexuality, especially female sexuality with a possible allusion to blood and menstruation

- the archaic word 'thou' may remind you of biblical language, and the Fall from Eden with its sexual overtones.

4 The socialist political context

Blake was horrified by social conditions in London, and expressed views which today could be called 'socialist'. Here are two stanzas from 'London' in which Blake exemplifies the 'mind-forg'd manacles' of the society of his day. These manacles may have been created by powerful people such as the wealthy mill-owners, but perhaps also by philosophers who justified this sort of society.

How the Chimney-sweepers cry
Every blackning Church appalls,
And the hapless Soldiers sigh
Runs in blood down Palace walls

But most thro' midnight streets I hear
How the youthful Harlots curse
Blasts the new-born Infants tear
And blights with plagues the Marriage hearse

ACTIVITY 10

1 Is there a sense of great deprivation in this poem? Do the groups of people mentioned here have rights?

2 What is Blake's attitude to the authority of kings? And to the Church?

3 How many different groups of people are involved in this poem?

4 Looking at the whole poem, why does Blake call the streets 'charter'd'?

ACTIVITY 11

How the presentation develops this context:

1 What effect is created by the use of the first person as the speaker?

2 Think about the register:

   • look at verbs, such as 'cry', 'sigh', 'curse', 'tear'

   • look at adjectives, such as 'blackning', 'hapless', 'youthful'.

   How do they help to create the sense of oppression of the individual?

3 What is the effect of the image of the 'Marriage hearse'?

4 Why do the Chimney-sweepers cry?

5 What does 'mind-forg'd manacles' mean to you?

5 The psychological context

In the discussion of 'The Sick Rose' in Activity 7 you were given an example of a psychological/sexual reading of the poem. Now read 'A Poison Tree' – another poem by Blake – and work out how Blake creates a myth about jealousy with a psychological insight into the fragility of human friendships.

ACTIVITY 12

1 Begin by working out links between the poison tree of the poem, and the tree from the Garden of Eden.

   • What sort of fruit do both trees bear?

   • Is there any similarity between the outcome of the poem and what happens to Eve in the Garden of Eden? What are the differences?

2 How far do you think Blake is trying to rewrite the biblical myth?

6 The philosophical context

To consider this context, read the poem 'To Tirzah'.

ACTIVITY 13

1 Who or what is Tirzah?

2 Is there an echo of the Fall from Eden in the second and third stanzas?

3 Does Blake find a solution to the problems in the fourth stanza?

4 After the darkness of the *Songs of Experience*, has Blake found a way through the difficulties of physical and spiritual life for his contemporary society?

5 Unlike the myth in 'A Poison Tree', does 'To Tirzah' offer some hope? Or not?

Blake's engravings also form a context, in that he seemed to want to make the experiences conveyed by the poems as concrete as possible. Perhaps he was suggesting that experience should be considered in physical as well as abstract terms. He may also have felt that the expression of the experiences he wished to convey would be reinforced by using two mediums.

This study of contexts in Blake's poetry is not exhaustive. The biographical context is evident throughout many of the poems, since Blake lived in London and witnessed many of the events and situations he described.

Using this model framework, you can go on to explore other contexts related to *Songs of Innocence* and *Songs of Experience*.

Selected Poems by John Keats

John Keats kept returning in his poetry to certain key ideas:

- how mankind comes to terms with the imperfections of existence
- the relationship of 'real' life to art
- the search for truth in the life of a poet.

As Keats believed that everything of beauty carries with it the seeds of its own decay, the nature of his vision is inevitably tragic. But this idea is conveyed through extremely sensuous language so that, whilst the vision may be tragic, the expression of it is richly beautiful. Keats was influenced by Greek writers and artists because he believed strongly that they addressed similar issues.

Six contexts will be explored here:

1 The literary and historical contexts of the Romantic poet.

2 The context of nature.

3 The social, literary and historical contexts – the positive aspect of love.

4 The social context – the negative aspect of love.

5 The literary context – the suffering and alienation of the Romantic poet.

6 The philosophical context – the nature of the human condition.

1 The literary and historical contexts of the Romantic poet

In his poem 'Ode to a Nightingale', Keats describes the actual moment when he had his poetic vision. The speaker says that he is not helped by wine – 'charioted by **Bacchus**' but flies 'on the viewless wings of Poesy'.

In the fourth and fifth stanzas you read of the moments of vision:

> But here there is no light,
> Save what from heaven is with the breezes blown [. . .]
>
> I cannot see what flowers are at my feet,
>   Nor what soft incense hangs upon the boughs,
> But, in embalmèd darkness, guess each sweet [. . .]

ACTIVITY 1

1 What are the two main registers that Keats uses in these lines?

2 What impression is Keats trying to convey by references to 'heaven', 'incense', 'embalmèd'?

3 What might these references suggest about the poet's attitude to poetry?

4 In these lines, and in the rest of the stanza, how many of the senses does Keats refer to? What is he trying to convey through this sensual imagery?

5 Is there evidence here of Keats's idea of **negative capability** – of accepting experience without the need for proof or reason, of being able to live in a state of uncertainty?

Then in the seventh stanza the poet refers to the nightingale's immortal song:

> The same that oft-times hath
> Charm'd magic casements, opening on the foam
>   Of perilous seas, in faery lands forlorn.

ACTIVITY 2

1 How do you think the song of the nightingale could be compared to poetry?

2 What do you think that the 'magic casements' might be?

3 What do the 'faery lands' suggest? Think about the poet's visions.

In the next stanza, Keats picks up and repeats the word 'forlorn' as he says 'Adieu' to his moment of vision. The sound of the nightingale fades, as the poet asks at the end of the poem:

Was it a vision, or a waking dream?
   Fled is that music: – do I wake or sleep?

ACTIVITY 3

1   Do you think that the poet has come back to reality after his vision? Think about the contradictions or **paradoxes** which Keats expresses in his poetry:

   • that sadness inevitably accompanies moments of vision

   • that everything beautiful is destined to die

   • that sadness and joy are inseparably linked in the poet's mind and also in the human condition.

2   Do these sum up Keats's Romantic perception of poetry?

In assessing these points you have evaluated the contextual significance.

ACTIVITY 4

How the language develops this context:

1   Look at the whole poem again and work out how Keats has used the natural and divine registers together to indicate his sense of the importance of poetic creation.

2   Work out the sequences of contrasted phrases such as 'faery lands'/'forlorn'. How do these help to develop the meaning?

3   How does Keats evoke the senses? What effect does this have on you?

You may link this poem with the other Odes if you want to show how Keats explores the human situation from different perspectives.

2 The context of nature

In his 'Ode to Autumn' we again see Keats's skill in describing nature, and also the way he sees his own relationship with nature. In the first two stanzas Keats describes the richness of autumn, later personified as a benevolent goddess. The tone then changes in the final stanza:

Where are the songs of Spring? Ay, where are they?
  Think not of them, thou hast thy music too,
    While barrèd clouds bloom the soft-dying day [. . .]
  Then in a wailful choir the small gnats mourn [. . .]
And full-grown lambs loud bleat from hilly bourn;
  Hedge-crickets sing; [. . .]
    And gathering swallows twitter in the skies.

ACTIVITY 5

1 What sights and sounds does Keats pick out in these lines?

2 What sort of feeling do you think he is conveying?

3 Is there a hint here of the inevitability of decay?

ACTIVITY 6

How the language develops this context:

1 Look at the verbs used: 'mourn', 'bleat', 'sing'. What effect is created?

2 Look at the adjectives here and elsewhere in the poem, such as 'small', 'barrèd', 'wailful'. What effects are created?

3 Does any specific image from the poem strike you?

4 Why are the swallows 'gathering'?

5 Do the 'songs of Spring' refer to the songs of the poet?

6 Is there any sense here that life is transitory? And that the poetic vision might also be a fleeting experience?

3 Social, literary and historical contexts – the positive aspect of love

Within these contexts, explored through a reading of 'The Eve of St Agnes', we can look at Keats's attitude to the positive aspect of human love, and his use of the medieval world to portray this.

The positive aspect of human love

Read the opening stanza of 'The Eve of St Agnes'. Keats establishes a specific atmosphere right at the start of the poem.

ACTIVITY 7

1 How does Keats use the senses to convey a picture of the natural world?

2 Why is the natural world frozen? Is it just because it is winter or is this a metaphor for something else?

3 Is the human world frozen too?

4 From your knowledge of the whole poem, how does this relate to the idea that the experience of love is needed to awaken the emotions?

Keats may be seen to describe this awakening when Madeline and Porphyro are united as lovers in stanzas 30 and 35. At first Madeline is described:

And still she slept an azure-lidded sleep,
In blanchèd linen, smooth, and lavender'd [. . .]

And then Madeline describes Porphyro:

How changed thou art! how pallid, chill, and drear!
Give me that voice again, my Porphyro,
Those looks immortal, those complainings dear!

ACTIVITY 8

1 What aspects of the two lovers are stressed in these descriptions?

2 Do these remind you of the description of nature in the first stanza?

The change brought about by love is clear. Porphyro is described in stanza 36 as:

Ethereal, flush'd, and like a throbbing star [. . .]

ACTIVITY 9

1 What differences are there now in the presentation of Porphyro?

2 Is Keats suggesting that these are the effects of love? And that the experience of love brings human beings to life?

Keats takes this attitude further. In the third stanza he continues with his description of the **Beadsman**, introduced in the first stanza:

But no – already had his death-bell rung; [. . .]

And finally you are told of the Beadsman's death in the final stanza:

> The Beadsman, after thousand **aves** told,
> For aye unsought-for slept among his ashes cold.

ACTIVITY 10

1 What sort of death does the Beadsman die? Does anybody care about him?

2 Do you think this might be a comment on the futility of orthodox religion?

3 What, then, is Keats saying about the experience of love?

Look at the account of Angela's death in the final stanza. She, too, dies 'with meagre face deform'.

ACTIVITY 11

1 What does the word 'meagre' suggest to you?

2 Does Angela live in a way similar to the Beadsman?

In the social context, Keats seems to be stressing the importance of the experience of human love and suggesting that love somehow defeats mortality.

The literary and historical contexts – the medieval world

Look at how Keats makes use of the medieval world, evident in the rich descriptions throughout the poem. Read through stanzas 24–6.

ACTIVITY 12

1 How does Keats build up the richness of these scenes? Explore the ways in which he uses the senses.

2 What are the particular qualities of medieval life that Keats emphasises here? To help you, look at the print of William Holman Hunt's painting *Isabella or The Pot of Basil* on page 81.

3 What aspects of Keats's poetry might have inspired Pre-Raphaelite painters such as Holman Hunt?

4 How does Keats use the **medievalism** to explore the value of the past? Does he think that everything in the past is of value? Think about the way Madeline and Porphyro flee from their pasts.

5 Is **orthodox** religion one of the elements which Keats rejects?

This activity draws all three contexts – social, literary and historical – together.

4 The social context – the negative aspect of love

To begin exploring this aspect you could use the narrative poem 'Isabella or The Pot of Basil'. Many readers see this poem as the reverse of 'The Eve of St Agnes'. At first, Keats appears to present the lovers in a similar way to 'The Eve of St Agnes'. In the fourth and fifth stanzas he describes the lovers before they can consummate their love:

A whole long month of May in this sad plight
    Made their cheeks paler by the break of June: [. . .]
Honeyless days and days did he let pass;

Until sweet Isabella's untouch'd cheek
    Fell sick within the rose's just domain, [. . .]

ACTIVITY 13

1 How does Keats show the state of mind of the undeclared lovers?

2 What normally happens in nature in the months of May and June?

3 Why do you think he uses the words 'honeyless' and 'untouch'd'?

4 What might Keats be suggesting about human beings living without love?

As in 'The Eve of St Agnes', love is seen to bring changes, in the ninth stanza:

'Love: thou art leading me from wintry cold,
    Lady! thou leadest me to summer clime,
And I must taste the blossoms that unfold
    In its ripe warmth this gracious morning time.'

Isabella and the Pot of Basil by William Holman Hunt

ACTIVITY 14

1 What changes can you see in the lovers now?

2 How does Keats make use of the senses here?

3 What might the use of the word 'gracious' suggest?

Later on, this poem differs from 'The Eve of St Agnes'. The mercenary brothers kill Lorenzo, and finally Isabella retrieves his head, burying it in her pot of basil. Keats describes Isabella in stanza 52:

And she forgot the stars, the moon, and sun,
    And she forgot the blue above the trees, [. . .]
    And the new morn she saw not: but in peace
Hung over her sweet Basil evermore,
And moisten'd it with tears unto the core.

ACTIVITY 15

How the presentation develops the social context:

1 What has happened to Isabella now? How is she presented here? Think about Keats's use of the senses in his descriptions.

2 Do these lines, and the stanza as a whole, present a reversal of the earlier stanzas you looked at?

3 Could the word 'peace' be ironical? Is it more of a death-like peace?

4 What is Keats suggesting in this poem? Must there be tragedy in our lives as well as happiness?

5 The literary context – the suffering and alienation of the Romantic poet

To look at another aspect of the literary context, read the poem 'The Fall of Hyperion'.

ACTIVITY 16

• Begin by working out what the opposed gods, Saturn and Apollo, represent.

• Comparing this poem with 'Ode to a Nightingale', does Keats present the same vision of the Romantic poet in both poems, or is there more emphasis on suffering and alienation here?

6 The philosophical context – the nature of the human condition

To explore this context you could look at 'Ode on a Grecian Urn'. Here Keats presents to the reader the central conflicts in life.

ACTIVITY 17

1 Does Keats offer any solutions to the central conflicts in life?

3 Might Keats find beauty in bleak truth itself?

4 How else do *you* perceive the relationship between truth and beauty in this poem?

Now you have examined the six contexts here, you can go on to explore others on your own.

Internet sites

British literature http://www.britishliterature.com/

English teaching in the United Kingdom
http://www.ourworld.compuserve.com/homepages/harry_dodds/

Literary resources on the net http://www.andromeda.rutgers.edu/-jlynch/lit

CD-ROMs

Silver Hooks and Golden Sands (An Introduction to Poetry and Prose in English 1360–1900)

The English Romantic Poets
Both from Headstrong Interactive, Magdale House, Lea Lane, Netherton, Huddersfield, HD4 7DL.

Select bibliography

General textbooks

Cambridge Companion to English Literature, 1500–1600 (Cambridge University Press, 2000)

The New Pelican Guide to English Literature, ed. Boris Ford: *The Age of Shakespeare* (Penguin) revised and expanded edn 1982

Drama

William Shakespeare – *Plays*

General reading

Themes and Conventions of Elizabethan Tragedy, M. C. Bradbrook (Cambridge University Press, 1969)

The Problem Plays of Shakespeare: a study of Julius Caesar, Measure for Measure, Anthony and Cleopatra, Ernest Schantzer (1963)

The Wheel of Fire, G. Wilson Knight (Routledge & Kegan Paul, 1930 repr. 1959)

Shakespeare's Language, Frank Kermode (Penguin, 2001)

Othello

Aspects of Othello, eds Muir and Edwards (Cambridge University Press, 1981)

Othello. A casebook, John Wain (Macmillan. 1971)

Shakespeare's Tragic Sequence, Kenneth Muir (Hutchinson University Library, 1972)

Henry IV Part 2

Henry IV Parts I and II. A casebook, G. K. Hunter (Macmillan, 1970)

Shakespeare's History Plays, Richard II *to* Henry V, New Casebooks, ed. G. Holderness (Macmillan, 1992)

Shakespeare: The Histories, ed. Eugene M. Waith (Prentice-Hall, 1965)

The Merchant of Venice

The Merchant of Venice, A casebook, John Wilders (Macmillan)

A Natural Perspective, Northrop Frye (Colombia University Press, 1965)

Shakespeare's Happy Comedies, John Dover Wilson (Faber, 1962)

The Wakefield Master

Noah and his Sons, The Second Shepherd's Play, and Herod the Great: English Folk-play, E. K. Chambers (Oxford University Press, 1933)

The Medieval Stage, E. K. Chambers (Classic Books, 1903)

Medieval English Drama. A casebook, Peter Happé (Macmillan, 1984)

John Webster – *The Duchess of Malfi*

The White Devil and the Duchess of Malfi. A casebook, ed. R. V. Holdsworth (Macmillan, 1975)

The White Devil and The Duchess of Malfi, John D. Jump (Blackwell, 1970)

John Webster: A Critical Study, Clifford Leech (Hogarth Press, 1951)

Themes and Conventions of Elizabethan Tragedy, M. C. Bradbrook (Cambridge University Press, 1969)

Ben Jonson – *Volpone*

Jonson: Volpone. A casebook, Jonas A. Barish (Macmillan, 1972)

The Jacobean Drama, an Interpretation, Una Ellis-Fermor (Methuen, 1961)

Jacobean Theatre, Stratford-Upon-Avon Studies, eds John Russell Brown and Bernard Harris (Arnold, 1965)

Poetry

Women Romantic Poets

The Singing Swan: An Account of Anna Seward, Margaret Ashmun (London University Press, 1931)

Dorothy Wordsworth and Romanticism, Susan M. Levin (Rutgers, The State University, 1987)

The Bluestocking Circle: Women, Friendship, and the Life of the Mind in Eighteenth Century England, Sylvia Harcstarck Myers (Oxford University Press, 1991)

The Muses of Resistance: Labouring Class Women's Poetry in Britain, 1739–1796, Donna Landry (Cambridge University Press, 1991)

Shakespeare's Sister: Feminist Essays on Women Poets, eds Sandra Gilbert and Susan Gubar (Indiana University Press, 1979)

The New Feminist Criticism: Essays on Women, Literature and Theory, Elaine Showalter (Virago, 1985)

William Wordsworth – *The Prelude*

The Prelude, 1799, 1805, 1850, eds. Jonathon Wordsworth, M. H. Abrams and Stephen Gill (Norton Critical Edition, 1979)

Wordsworth. A casebook, eds A. R. Jones and W. Tydeman (Macmillan, 1972)

Wordsworth, The Prelude. A casebook, eds W. J. Harvey and R. Gravil (Macmillan, 1972)

The Confessional Imagination: A Reading of Wordsworth's Prelude, Frank DeMay MacConnell (John Hopkins University Press, 1974)

William Blake – *Songs of Innocence and Songs of Experience*

William Blake, New Casebook, ed. David Putner (Macmillan, 1996)

The Romantic Imagination, John Spencer Hill (Macmillan, 1977)

English Romantic Poets. Modern essays in criticism, ed. M. H. Abrams (Oxford University Press, New York, 1975)

Natural Supernaturalism, Tradition and Revolution in Romantic Literature, M. H. Abrams (Oxford University Press, New York, 1971)

Selected Poems – John Keats

John Keats, The Living Year, Robert Gittings (Heinemann, 1978)

Coleridge, Keats and Shelley, ed. P. J. Kitson (Macmillan, 1996)

John Keats, Odes. A casebook, G. S. Fraser (Macmillan, 1971)

Keats: The Narrative Poems. A casebook, ed. John Spencer Hill (Macmillan, 1983)

Module ⑤ Literary Connections

This module carries 30% of the final A2 mark and 15% of the final A Level mark. The marks are divided amongst the Assessment Objectives like this:

ASSESSMENT OBJECTIVES

AO1 communicate clearly the knowledge, understanding and insight appropriate to literary study, using appropriate terminology and accurate and coherent written expression
(5% of the final A2 mark; 2.5% of the final A Level mark)

AO2ii respond with knowledge and understanding to literary texts of different types and periods, exploring and commenting on relationships and comparisons between literary texts
(13% of the final A2 mark; 6.5% of the final A Level mark)

AO3 show detailed understanding of the ways in which writers' choices of form, structure and language shape meanings
(6% of the final A2 mark; 3% of the final A Level mark)

AO4 articulate independent opinions and judgements, informed by different interpretations of literary texts by other readers
(6% of the final A2 mark; 3% of the final A Level mark)

The purpose of this module

The aim of this module is to provide you with the opportunity to focus on the ways in which texts relate to each other, by comparing two texts. As you can see from the list of Assessment Objectives above, AO2ii is very important here. This means that whichever texts you use for this module, and however you tackle the module, you must keep the requirement to explore comparisons at the centre of your work.

There are two ways to use this module, as a coursework unit or as a written exam unit. Whichever you choose, one of the texts has to be a prose text. If you take the coursework unit, you can choose any texts you like, as long as at least one of them is prose, and both are suitable for A Level study. The choices have to be approved by AQA, however. If you opt for the written unit, you have to choose one of the options of paired texts set for the exam.

Whichever way you use the module, the important thing is to find and explore the relationships and comparisons between the texts. The first section will therefore look at ways in which you can start exploring comparisons. The second, third and fourth sections examine the two assessment methods.

Ways of looking at texts for comparison

Whether you are choosing your own texts for coursework or looking at set texts for the exam, it is important to identify at least two or three ways in which comparisons can be made, so that the individual texts are illuminated by the comparison. This is one of the central points of AO2ii: by looking at one text in the light of another, you come to understand more about it. A good way to think about similarities and differences between texts is to focus on the other Assessment Objectives. The ideas and related activities that follow are intended to offer you a wide range of possibilities for comparison.

Assessment Objective 3

> show detailed understanding of the ways in which writers' choices of form, structure and language shape meanings

Form

Form is an interesting starting point for comparison, as you can think about the ways that different forms deal with the same ideas. You could, for instance, compare the novel *Birdsong* by Sebastian Faulks and the war poetry of Wilfred Owen. These texts, or any two concerned with the First World War, would also prepare the way for Module 6, Reading for Meaning. The following activities begin by comparing form, but move on to other issues – you should try to do the same with your texts.

Below is a 'fragment' of a poem from *Wilfred Owen – The War Poems*:

FRAGMENT: CRAMPED IN THAT FUNNELLED HOLE

Cramped in that funnelled hole, they watched the dawn
Open a jagged rim around; a yawn
Of death's jaws, which had all but swallowed them
Stuck in the bottom of his throat of phlegm.

They were in one of many mouths of Hell
Not seen of seers in visions; only felt
As teeth of traps; when bones and the dead are smelt
Under the mud where long ago they fell
Mixed with the sour sharp odour of the shell.

In the following extract from *Birdsong*, Stephen, the main character in the novel, has taken refuge in a shell-hole during an attack:

Stephen dropped his face into the earth and let it fill his mouth. He closed his eyes because he had seen enough. You are going to hell. Azaire's parting words filled his head. They were drilled in by the shattering noise around them.

Byrne somehow got the boy back into the shellhole. Stephen wished he hadn't. He was clearly going to die.

Harrington's sergeant was shouting for another charge and a dozen men responded. Stephen watched them reach the first line of wire before he realized that Byrne was with them. He was trying to force a way through the wire when he was caught off the ground, suspended, his boots shaking as his body was filled with bullets.

Stephen lay in the shellhole with the boy and the man who had died in the morning. For three hours until the sun began to weaken he watched the boy begging for water. He tried to close his ears to the plea. On one corpse there was still a bottle, but a bullet hole had let most of it leak away. What was left was a reddish brown, contaminated by earth and blood. Stephen poured it into the boy's beseeching mouth.

ACTIVITY 1

Compare the two extracts above, using these questions to help you.

1 The *forms* are clearly different. The extract from the novel is exactly that. How do you know it is not complete in itself? What information might you expect to have been given before this point in the novel?

2 The poem is a fragment – it was found after Owen's death, and thought to be incomplete. Can it stand by itself, though? How is it different from the prose extract in this respect, and why? Do you need to know anything else? Think about the writer's intentions.

3 Owen creates some effects in this poem using structures not available to Faulks. Look at the second line in each stanza, where the end of a line naturally creates a gap. You might look at the rhymes, too – again not found in the prose passage.

4 The ideas and situations – part of the *context* of the writing here – are clearly comparable. Think about the status and rank of the speakers, their attitudes, the time of day, the noise, or lack of it.

5 The *language* used by each writer is revealing. Throughout the poem, Owen uses the idea that the shellhole is like a mouth. Find where the idea begins and trace it through, noticing how he uses the metaphor to comment on the soldiers' situation.

6 Although the prose is not as packed with imagery as the poem – a difference resulting from form, perhaps – Faulks does use language to convey images, and to create emotive effects. Look at the first and last lines of the extract with this in mind.

7 Both writers use the senses extensively to involve the reader. Look at the way they use sight, hearing, touch and smell.

8 What is the attitude of each of the writers to the war, do you think? Notice that they both use the same key word to describe the nature of the experience.

If you had chosen this pair of texts, the prose extract here might have led you to read other poems by Wilfred Owen for comparison: 'Anthem for Doomed Youth'; for example, or 'Inspection'.

Here are two more pairs of extracts to work on:

Pair 1

The opening four lines of 'Dulce Et Decorum Est', also by Wilfred Owen:

Bent double, like old beggars under sacks,
Knock-kneed, coughing like hags, we cursed through sludge,
Till on the haunting flares we turned our backs
And towards our distant rest began to trudge.

And a different passage from *Birdsong*:

It was dark at last. The night poured down in waves from the ridge above them and the guns at last fell silent.

The earth began to move. To their right a man who had lain still since the first attack, eased himself upright, then fell again when his damaged leg would not take his weight. Other single men moved, and began to come up like worms from their shellholes, limping, crawling, dragging themselves out. Within minutes the hillside was seething with the movement of the wounded as they attempted to get themselves back to their line.

'Christ,' said Weir, 'I had no idea there were so many men out there.'

It was like a resurrection in a cemetery twelve miles long. Bent, agonized shapes loomed in multitudes on the churned earth, limping and dragging back to reclaim their life. It was as though the land were disgorging a generation of crippled sleepers, each one distinct but related to its twisted brothers as they teemed up from the reluctant earth.

Pair 2

The first fourteen and last five lines from 'Strange Meeting', by Wilfred Owen:

It seemed that out of battle I escaped
Down some profound dull tunnel, long since scooped
Through granites which titanic wars had groined.

Yet also there encumbered sleepers groaned,
Too fast in thought or death to be bestirred.
Then, as I probed them, one sprang up, and stared
With piteous recognition in fixed eyes,
Lifting distressful hands, as if to bless.
And by his smile, I knew that sullen hall, –
By his dead smile I knew we stood in Hell.

With a thousand pains that vision's face was grained;
Yet no blood reached there from the upper ground,
And no guns thumped, or down the flues made moan.
'Strange friend,' I said, 'here is no cause to mourn.'

[. . .]

'I am the enemy you killed, my friend.
I knew you in this dark: for so you frowned
Yesterday through me as you jabbed and killed.
I parried; but my hands were loath and cold.
Let us sleep now. . . .'

The following extract from *Birdsong* falls at the end of a chapter, and almost at the end of the account of First World War experience in the novel. Stephen is pulled from a blown-up tunnel by a German soldier, who has also been trapped underground:

He looked up and saw the legs of his rescuer. They were clothed in the German *feldgrau*, the colour of his darkest dream.

He staggered to his feet and his hand went to pull out his revolver, but there was nothing there, only the torn, drenched rags of his trousers.

He looked into the face of the man who stood in front of him and his fists went up from his sides like those of a farm boy about to fight.

At some deep level, far below anything his exhausted mind could reach, the conflicts of his soul dragged through him like waves grating on the packed shingle of a beach. The sound of his life calling to him on a distant road; the faces of the men who had been slaughtered, the closed eyes of Michael Weir in his coffin; his scalding hatred of the enemy, of Max and all the men who had brought him to this moment; the flesh and love of Isabelle, and the eyes of her sister.

Far beyond thought, the resolution came to him and he found his arms, still raised, beginning to spread and open.

Levi looked at this wild-eyed figure, half-demented, his brother's killer. For no reason he could tell, he found that he had opened his own arms in turn, and the two men fell upon each other's shoulders, weeping at the bitter strangeness of their human lives.

ACTIVITY 2

Pair 1:

1 Consider how the use of dialogue in the prose passage adds to the effect.

2 Compare the imagery used in the two extracts, noticing the intensity of the images in *Birdsong* this time.

3 Look for words and phrases in the two extracts which are the same or very similar. Why do both writers make these choices, do you think?

4 Compare the situations and the writers' attitudes.

The prose passage might also lead you to look at 'At a Calvary near the Ancre', by Wilfred Owen, if you had chosen this pair of texts.

Pair 2:

5 There is a lot to say about the effects of the different forms here. In the poem, look at the **half-rhymes** and how these add to the impact and the effect produced by the last line. The prose passage also has a finality about it – in what way does it read like an ending? Putting the two together, you can compare the different effects of form.

6 Both language and situations are similar here. Compare them closely. The similarities should reveal something about the attitudes and intentions of the writers.

7 What futures are suggested in each of these endings?

Now look at the section on Coursework on page 120, and you'll see how this sort of comparison can be applied to complete texts.

Structure

Structure can be an important factor in making comparisons between texts. For instance, four novels which all deal with war, but which differ significantly in structure, are *Birdsong*, Joseph Heller's *Catch-22*, Martin Amis's *Time's Arrow*, and J. G. Farrell's *The Siege of Krishnapur*. Although the central subject of each novel is war, there are some significant differences in the structures chosen by the writers to present it. Only *The Siege of Krishnapur* is a straightforward chronological narrative. Although *Birdsong* is chronological through the war episodes, there are significant leaps of time, and a late twentieth-century narrative is interwoven with the 1914–18 episodes. *Catch-22* offers characters' names rather than numbers as chapter headings, when that character is the focus of the chapter. Although there is time development, it has to be pieced together by the reader, and it returns to the same incident several times. *Time's Arrow* is chronological in the sense that it tells the story of the Holocaust backwards, each chapter starting at a point before the previous one.

If any two of these novels were chosen as texts to compare, a key element would be the effects of these choices of structure: how the writers 'shape meanings' from their choices, to echo the words of the Assessment Objective. The contexts could also be compared, as well as the writers' attitudes, which might be conveyed by language as well as structure. You could also think about which approach you found most effective, to enable you to address AO4.

Language

Language is a key point of focus when comparing texts. There are texts, for instance, where dialect is a significant factor. Irving Welsh's *Trainspotting*, for instance, could be compared with Peter Roper's play *The Steamie*, also set in Glasgow, or with any of Roddy Doyle's 'Barrytown' novels. The social and cultural contexts are different in each. Language change across time could also be looked at, if two texts from very different time periods were studied. Nathaniel Hawthorne's *The Scarlet Letter*, for example, which deals with the consequences of adultery, could be compared with A. S. Byatt's *Possession*, which within itself has contrasting forms and different language registers to reflect language changes across time.

Activity 3 focuses on similarities and differences in language. In each text, the writer is showing significant moments in the lives of the central characters, and is trying to convey the nature of joy using a range of techniques.

In this extract from *Sons and Lovers*, by D. H. Lawrence, Miriam Leivers takes Paul Morel to see a bush which she admires.

He followed her across the nibbled pasture in the dusk. There was a coolness in the wood, a scent of leaves, of honeysuckle, and a twilight. The two walked in silence. Night came wonderfully there, among the throng of dark-trunks. He looked round, expectant.

She wanted to show him a certain wild-rose bush she had discovered. She knew it was wonderful. And yet, till he had seen it, she felt it had not come into her soul. Only he could make it her own, immortal. She was dissatisfied.

Dew was already on the paths. In the old-oak wood a mist was rising, and he hesitated, wondering whether one whiteness were a strand of fog or only campion-flowers pallid in a cloud.

By the time they came to the pine-trees Miriam was getting very eager and very intense. Her bush might be gone. She might not be able to find it; and she wanted it so much. Almost passionately she wanted to be with him when he stood before the flowers. They were going to have a communion together – something that thrilled her, something holy. He was walking beside her in silence. They were very near to each other. She trembled, and he listened, vaguely anxious.

Coming to the edge of the wood, they saw the sky in front, like mother-of-pearl, and the earth growing dark. Somewhere on the outermost branches of the pine-wood the honeysuckle was streaming scent.

'Where?' he asked.

'Down the middle path,' she murmured, quivering.

When they turned the corner of the path she stood still. In the wide walk between the pines, gazing rather frightened, she could distinguish nothing for some moments; the greying light robbed things of their colour. Then she saw her bush.

'Ah!' she cried, hastening forward.

It was very still. The tree was tall and straggling. It had thrown its briers over a hawthorn-bush, and its long streamers trailed thick right down to the grass, splashing the darkness everywhere with great split stars, pure white. In bosses of ivory and in large splashed stars the roses gleamed on the darkness of foliage and stems and grass. Paul and Miriam stood close together, silent, and watched. Point after point the steady roses shone out of them, seeming to kindle something in their souls. The dusk came like smoke around, and still did not put out the roses.

Paul looked into Miriam's eyes. She was pale and expectant with wonder, her lips were parted, and her dark eyes lay open to him. His look seemed to travel down into her. Her soul quivered. It was the communion she wanted. He turned aside, as if pained. He turned to the bush.

'They seems as if they walk like butterflies, and shake themselves,' he said.

She looked at her roses. They were white, some incurved and holy, others expanded in an ecstasy. The tree was dark as a shadow. She lifted her hand impulsively to the flowers; she went forward and touched them in worship.

'Let us go,' he said.

There was a cool scent of ivory roses – a white, virgin scent. Something made him feel anxious and imprisoned. The two walked in silence.

'Till Sunday,' he said quietly, and left her; and she walked home slowly, feeling her soul satisfied with the holiness of the night. He stumbled down the path. And as soon as he was out of the wood, in the free open meadow, where he could breathe, he started to run as fast as he could. It was like a delicious delirium in his veins.

In this extract from *To the Lighthouse* by Virginia Woolf, Mrs Ramsay is serving a meal to her guests, and feels that the coherence she had wanted has happened at last:

Everything seemed possible. Everything seemed right. Just now (but this cannot last, she thought, dissociating herself from the moment while they were all talking about boots) just now she had reached security; she hovered like a hawk suspended; like a flag floated in an element of joy which filled every nerve of her body fully and sweetly, not noisily, solemnly rather, for it arose, she thought, looking at them all eating there, from husband and children and friends; all of which rising in this profound stillness (she was helping William Bankes to one very small piece more and peered into the depths of the earthenware pot) seemed now for no special reason to stay there like a smoke, like a fume rising upwards, holding them safe together. Nothing need be said; nothing could be said. There it was, all round them. It partook, she felt, carefully helping Mr Bankes to a specially tender piece, of eternity; as she had already felt about something different once before that afternoon; there is a coherence in things, a stability; something, she meant, is immune from change, and shines out (she glanced at the window with its ripple of reflected lights) in the face of the flowing, the fleeting, the spectral, like a ruby; so that again tonight she had the feeling she had had once today already, of peace, of rest. Of such moments, she thought, the thing is made that remains for ever after. This would remain.

'Yes,' she assured William Bankes, 'there is plenty for everybody.'

ACTIVITY 3

1 Compare the physical effects of joy on the characters in the extracts.

2 Both writers suggest that the characters feel something beyond and above their own physical sensations. How does each writer try to convey this idea?

3 Look for descriptions of movement and stillness in each piece, and how they are conveyed. You should look particularly for repetition of words and **syntax,** and sentence lengths.

4 Look for reference to:

   • religion

   • sexuality

   • light and colour

   • humour, or seriousness.

   This might help you to sum up the differences between the two extracts. How are the tones of the extracts different? What do you conclude about the writers' intentions?

Language is a key feature in both of these texts. If you were comparing the two texts, you could look at:

• the way each writer conveys childhood

• sentence forms

• differences in structure

• invented language.

Meanings

The central meaning of texts could obviously form a basis for comparison, but if you are choosing texts for coursework it would be better to choose texts where the links and comparisons could be developed into other areas. A 'rites of passage' novel like *A Portrait of the Artist as a Young Man*, could be compared to another novel, such as J. D. Salinger's *The Catcher in the Rye*. The phrase 'rites of passage' refers to key times in people's lives when common experiences such as birth, marriage and death have to be dealt with. In literature, 'rites of passage' often refers to experiences which highlight the joys and difficulties of adolescence, as teenagers move towards the adult world. These 'rites' might concern spiritual or political awareness, exploration, independence, or sexual drive.

Activity 4 takes another extract from *Sons and Lovers* by D. H. Lawrence, this time for comparison with an extract from *A Suitable Boy*, by Vikram Seth. Texts can be compared in a number of ways of course, with the same or other texts.

In this extract from *Sons and Lovers*, Miriam Leivers is attracted to Paul Morel. They are both in their teens:

Paul had been many times up to Willey Farm during the autumn. He was friends with the two youngest boys. Edgar, the eldest, would not condescend at first. And Miriam also refused to be approached. She was afraid of being set at nought, as by her own brothers. The girl was romantic in her soul. Everywhere was a Walter Scott heroine being loved by men with helmets or with plumes in their caps. She herself was something of a princess turned into a swine-girl in her own imagination. And she was afraid lest this boy, who, nevertheless, looked something like a Walter Scott hero, who could paint and speak French, and knew what algebra meant, and who went by train to Nottingham every day, might consider her simply as the swine-girl, unable to perceive the princess beneath; so she held aloof.

Her great companion was her mother. They were both brown-eyed, and inclined to be mystical, such women as treasure religion inside them, breathe it in their nostrils, and see the whole of life in a mist thereof. So to Miriam, Christ and God made one great figure, which she loved tremblingly and passionately when a tremendous sunset burned out the western sky, and Ediths, and Lucys, and Rowenas, Brian de Bois Guilberts, Rob Roys, and Guy Mannerings, rustled the sunny leaves in the morning, or sat in her bedroom aloft, alone, when it snowed. That was life to her. For the rest, she drudged in the house, which work she would not have minded had not her clean red floor been mucked up immediately by the trampling farm-boots of her brothers. She madly wanted her little brother of four to let her swathe him and stifle him in her love; she went to church reverently, with bowed head, and quivered in anguish from the vulgarity of the other choir-girls and from the common-sounding voice of the curate; she fought with her brothers, whom she considered brutal louts; and she held not her father in too high esteem because he did not carry any mystical ideals cherished in his heart but only wanted to have as easy a time as he could, and his meals when he was ready for them.

She hated her position as swine-girl. She wanted to be considered. She wanted to learn, thinking that if she could read, as Paul said he could read, 'Colomba', or the 'Voyage autour de ma Chambre' the world would have a different face for her and a deepened respect. She could not be princess by wealth or standing. So she was mad to have learning whereon to pride herself. For she was different from other folk, and must not be scooped up among the common fry. Learning was the only distinction to which she thought to aspire.

Her beauty – that of a shy, wild, quiveringly sensitive thing – seemed nothing to her. Even her soul, so strong for rhapsody, was not enough. She must have something to reinforce her pride, because she felt different from other people. Paul she eyed rather wistfully. On the whole, she scorned the male sex. But here was a new specimen, quick, light, graceful, who could be gentle and who could be sad, and who was clever, and who knew a lot, and who had a death in the family. The boy's poor morsel of learning exalted him almost sky-high in her esteem. Yet she tried hard to scorn him, because he would not see in her the princess but only the swine-girl. And he scarcely observed her.

Then he was so ill, and she felt he would be weak. Then she would be stronger than he. Then she could love him. If she could be mistress of him in his weakness, take care of him, if he could depend on her, if she could, as it were, have him in her arms, how she could love him!

This is the opening of Vikram Seth's novel *A Suitable Boy*, set in India. It was first published in 1993.

'You too will marry a boy I choose,' said Mrs Rupa Mehra firmly to her younger daughter.

Lata avoided the maternal imperative by looking around the great lamp-lit garden of Prem Nivas. The wedding-guests were gathered on the lawn. 'Hmm,' she said. This annoyed her mother further.

'I know what your hmms mean, young lady, and I can tell you I will not stand for hmms in this matter. I do know what is best. I am doing it all for you. Do you think it is easy for me, trying to arrange things for all four of my children without His help?' Her nose began to redden at the thought of her husband, who would, she felt certain, be partaking of their present joy from somewhere benevolently above. Mrs Rupa Mehra believed, of course, in reincarnation, but at moments of exceptional sentiment, she imagined that the late Rughubir Mehra still inhabited the form in which she had known him when he was alive: the robust, cheerful form of his early forties before overwork had brought about his heart attack at the height of the Second World War. Eight years ago, eight years, thought Mrs Rupa Mehra miserably.

'Now, now, Ma, you can't cry on Savita's wedding day,' said Lata, putting her arm gently but not very concernedly around her mother's shoulder.

'If He had been here, I could have worn the tissue-patola sari I wore for my own wedding,' sighed Mrs Rupa Mehra. 'But it is too rich for a widow to wear.'

'Ma!' said Lata, a little exasperated at the emotional capital her mother insisted on making out of every possible circumstance. 'People are looking at you. They want to congratulate you, and they'll think it very odd if they see you crying in this way.'

Several guests were indeed doing namasté to Mrs Rupa Mehra and smiling at her; the cream of Brahmpur society, she was pleased to note.

'Let them see me!' said Mrs Rupa Mehra defiantly, dabbing at her eyes hastily with a handkerchief perfumed with 4711 eau-de-Cologne. 'They will only think it is because of my happiness at Savita's wedding. Everything I do is for you, and no one appreciates me. I have chosen such a good boy for Savita, and all everyone does is complain.'

Lata reflected that of the four brothers and sisters, the only one who hadn't complained of the match had been the sweet-tempered, fair-complexioned, beautiful Savita herself.

'He is a little thin, Ma,' said Lata, a bit thoughtlessly. This was putting it mildly. Pran Kapoor, soon to be her brother-in-law, was lank, dark, gangly, and asthmatic.

'Thin? What is thin? Everyone is trying to become thin these days. Even I have had to fast the whole day and it is not good for my diabetes. And if Savita is not complaining, everyone should be happy with him. Arun and Varun are always complaining: why didn't they choose a boy for their sister then? Pran is a good, decent, cultured khatri boy.'

There was no denying that Pran, at thirty, was a good boy, a decent boy, and belonged to the right caste. And, indeed, Lata did like Pran. Oddly enough, she knew him better than her sister did – or, at least, had seen him for longer than her sister had. Lata was studying English at Brahmpur University, and Pran Kapoor was a popular lecturer there. Lata had attended his class on the Elizabethans, while Savita, the bride, had met him for only an hour, and that too in her mother's company.

'And Savita will fatten him up,' added Mrs Rupa Mehra. 'Why are you trying to annoy me when I am so happy? And Pran and Savita will be happy, you will see. They will be happy,' she continued emphatically. 'Thank you, thank you,' she now beamed at those who were coming up to greet her. 'It is so wonderful – the boy of my dreams, and such a good family. The Minister Sahib has been very kind to us. And Savita is so happy. Please eat something, please eat: they have made such delicious gulab-jamuns, but owing to my diabetes I cannot eat them even after the ceremonies. I am not even allowed gajak, which is so difficult to resist in winter. But please eat, please eat. I must go in to check what is happening: the time that the pandits have given is coming up, and there is no sign of either bride or groom!' She looked at Lata, frowning. Her younger daughter was going to prove more difficult than her elder, she decided.

ACTIVITY 4

1   The basis for comparison here is 'rites of passage'. Begin by comparing and contrasting the preoccupations of the characters in the two extracts. Think about the events that take place, the lives and states of mind of the characters, their expectations and the nature of the 'rites of passage' being referred to. Notice that several are evoked in the second passage.

2   Now contrast the ways meanings are conveyed in the two extracts. Look at the diction of each extract, and the tone – which extract has humour, and how is it conveyed? Examine how Miriam's character is presented in the first extract, and the character of Mrs Rupa Mehra in the second. Look at narrative viewpoint, too. Compare the ways the single viewpoint is given in the first extract with the ways the two viewpoints are conveyed in the second.

3   The contexts of the writing are quite different – the first text was published in 1913, and the second in 1993. The first is set in England, and the second in India. Both have strong religious elements – how are they different? There are social and cultural contexts too. Look for the influence of these contexts in the details and language of the extracts, considering what are the most important contextual influences.

4   Now you could write a comparison of the two extracts.

Alternatively, a play could be chosen for comparison with a 'rites of passage' novel – perhaps Neil Simon's *Brighton Beach Memoirs* or *Broadway Bound*. In this case, differences of form in dealing with a similar subject could be analysed as well, as you did in Activities 1 and 2 on *Birdsong* and the war poems of Wilfred Owen.

Assessment Objective 4

> articulate independent opinions and judgements, informed by different interpretations of literary texts by other readers

Thinking about critical stances can be a good starting point for comparisons. One of the ways of interpreting texts such as *The Color Purple* by Alice Walker and *Oranges Are Not the Only Fruit* by Jeanette Winterson is to see them from a feminist perspective.

In this letter from *The Color Purple*, Celie is describing the preparations for Sofia's mother's funeral:

Harpo say, Whoever heard of women pallbearers. That all I'm trying to say.

Well, said Sofia, you said it. Now you can hush.

I know she your mother, say Harpo. But still.

You gon help us or not? say Sofia.

What it gon look like? say Harpo. Three big stout women pallbearers look like they ought to be home frying chicken.

Three of our brothers be with us, on the other side, say Sofia. I guess they look like field hands.

But peoples use to men doing this sort of thing. Women weaker, he say. People think they weaker, say they weaker, anyhow. Women spose to take it easy. Cry if you want to. Not try to take over.

Try to take over, say Sofia. The woman dead. I can cry and take it easy and lift the coffin too. And whether you help us or not with the food and the chairs and the get-together afterward, that's exactly what I plan to do.

In this extract from *Oranges Are Not the Only Fruit*, Jeanette, the central character, has started to preach in her church:

By Sunday the pastor had word back from the council. The real problem, it seemed, was going against the teachings of St Paul, and allowing women power in the church. Our branch of the church had never thought about it, we'd always had strong women, and the women organized everything. Some of us could preach, and quite plainly, in my case, the church was full because of it. There was uproar, then a curious thing happened. My mother stood up and said she believed this was right: that women had specific circumstances for their ministry, that the Sunday School was one of them, the Sisterhood another, but the message belonged to the men. Until this moment my life had still made some kind of sense. Now it was making no sense at all. My mother droned on about the importance of missionary work for a woman, that I was clearly such a woman, but had spurned my call in order to wield power on the home front, where it was inappropriate. She ended by saying that having taken on a man's world in other ways I had flouted God's law and tried to do it sexually. This was no spontaneous speech. She and the pastor had talked about it already. It was her weakness for the ministry that had done it. No doubt she'd told Pastor Spratt months ago. I looked around me. Good people, simple people, what would happen to them now? I knew my mother hoped I would blame myself, but I didn't. I knew now where the blame lay. If there's such a thing as spiritual adultery, my mother was a whore.

So there I was, my success in the pulpit being the reason for my downfall. The devil had attacked me at my weakest point: my inability to realize the limitations of my sex.

ACTIVITY 5

1 In the two extracts above, look for the similarities and differences in the ways that the two women's lives are limited by the societies they live in.

2 Are these limitations rules or customs? Look carefully for evidence from each extract.

3 What information is given in the extracts to help you to define the culture each woman lives in?

4 Compare the language used by Alice Walker and Jeanette Winterson.

A broader comparison of these two texts might include:

• the treatment of sexuality

• the ways that feminist issues are reflected in secondary narrative in each text – the letters from Africa in *The Color Purple*, and the developing myth in *Oranges Are Not the Only Fruit*

• the power struggles between male and female in the texts, and their very different outcomes.

The position of women in society could be an important element in looking at less overtly feminist texts. *The Scarlet Letter* by Nathaniel Hawthorne could be compared from this point of view with either Charlotte Brontë's *Jane Eyre* or Margaret Atwood's *The Handmaid's Tale*.

The presentation of power and class in texts – a Marxist perspective, in other words – could be another point of comparison to focus on. *Hard Times* by Charles Dickens and J. B. Priestley's play *An Inspector Calls* offer similar perspectives here, but in different social and historical contexts and in different forms. Read the extracts from these two texts below, and then work through the questions in Activity 6.

In this extract from *Hard Times*, 'millers' in the third paragraph refers to the mill-owners – the employers in Coketown:

A sunny midsummer day. There was such a thing sometimes, even in Coketown.

Seen from a distance in such weather, Coketown lay shrouded in a haze of its own, which appeared impervious to the sun's rays. You only knew the town was there, because you knew there could have been no such sulky blotch upon the prospect without a town. A blur of soot and smoke, now confusedly tending this way, now that way, now aspiring to the vault of Heaven, now murkily creeping along the earth, as the wind rose and fell, or changed its quarter: a dense formless jumble, with sheets of cross light in it, that showed nothing but masses of darkness: – Coketown in the distance was suggestive of itself, though not a brick of it could be seen.

The wonder was, it was there at all. It had been ruined so often, that it was amazing how it had borne so many shocks. Surely there never was such fragile china-ware as that of which the millers of Coketown were made. Handle them never so lightly, and they fell to pieces with such ease that you might suspect them of having been flawed before. They were ruined, when they were required to send labouring children to school; they were ruined, when inspectors were appointed to look into their works; they were ruined, when such inspectors considered it doubtful whether they were quite justified in chopping people up with their machinery; they were utterly undone, when it was hinted that perhaps they need not always make quite so much smoke. Besides Mr Bounderby's gold spoon which was generally received in Coketown, another prevalent fiction was very popular there. It took the form of a threat. Whenever a Coketowner felt he was ill-used – that is to say, whenever he was not left entirely alone, and it was proposed to hold him accountable for the consequences of any of his acts – he was sure to come out with the awful menace, that he would 'sooner pitch his property into the Atlantic'. This had terrified the Home Secretary within an inch of his life, on several occasions.

However, the Coketowners were so patriotic after all, that they had never pitched their property into the Atlantic yet, but on the contrary, had been kind enough to take mighty good care of it. So there it was, in the haze yonder; and it increased and multiplied.

In *An Inspector Calls*, a police inspector is visiting the house of the Birling family after the death of a girl called Eva Smith. During the visit he shows how each member of the family was in some way responsible for the death. In Extract A, he is dealing with Mr Birling, the owner of the factory in which Eva was employed. In Extract B, he leaves the house after exposing the complicity of all the family.

Extract A

BIRLING [. . .] and she'd been working in one of our machine shops for over a year. A good worker too. In fact, the foreman there told me he was ready to promote her into what we call a leading operator – head of a small group of girls. But after they came back from their holidays that August, they were all rather restless, and they suddenly decided to ask for more money. They were averaging about twenty-two and six, which was neither more nor less than the average in our industry. They wanted the rates raised so they could average about twenty-five shillings a week. I refused, of course.

INSPECTOR Why?

BIRLING [*surprised*] Did you say 'Why?'?

INSPECTOR	Yes. Why did you refuse?
BIRLING	Well, Inspector, I don't see that it's any concern of yours how I choose to run my business. Is it now?
INSPECTOR	It might be, you know.
BIRLING	I don't like that tone.
INSPECTOR	I'm sorry. But you asked me a question.
BIRLING	And you asked me a question before that, a quite unnecessary question too.
INSPECTOR	It's my duty to ask questions.
BIRLING	Well, it's my duty to keep labour costs down, and if I'd agreed to this demand for a new rate we'd have added about twelve per cent to our labour costs. Does that satisfy you? So I refused. Said I couldn't consider it. We were paying the usual rates and if they didn't like those rates, they could go and work somewhere else. It's a free country, I told them.
ERIC	It isn't if you can't go and work somewhere else.
INSPECTOR	Quite so.
BIRLING	[*to Eric*] Look – just you keep out of this. You hadn't even started in the works when this happened. So they went on strike. That didn't last long, of course.
GERALD	Not if it was just after the holidays. They'd all be broke – if I know them.
BIRLING	Right, Gerald. They mostly were. And so was the strike, after a week or two. Pitiful affair. Well, we let them all come back – at the old rates – except the four or five ring-leaders, who'd started the trouble. I went down myself and told them to clear out. And this girl, Eva Smith, was one of them. She'd had a lot to say – far too much – so she had to go.
GERALD	You couldn't have done anything else.
ERIC	He could. He could have kept her on instead of throwing her out. I call it tough luck.
BIRLING	Rubbish! If you don't come down sharply on some of these people, they'd soon be asking for the earth.
GERALD	I should say so!
INSPECTOR	They might. But after all it's better to ask for the earth than to take it.

Extract B

INSPECTOR [. . .] [*Rather savagely, to Birling.*] You started it. She wanted twenty-five shillings a week instead of twenty-two and sixpence. You made her pay a heavy price for that. And now she'll make you pay a heavier price still.

BIRLING [*unhappily*] Look, Inspector – I'd give thousands – yes, thousands –

INSPECTOR You're offering the money at the wrong time, Mr Birling.

[*He makes a move as if concluding the session, possibly shutting up notebook, etc. Then surveys them sardonically.*]

No, I don't think any of you will forget. Nor that young man, Croft, though he at least had some affection for her and made her happy for a time. Well, Eva Smith's gone. And you can't do her any good now, either. You can't even say 'I'm sorry, Eva Smith.'

SHEILA [*Who is crying quietly*] That's the worst of it.

INSPECTOR But just remember this. One Eva Smith has gone – but there are millions and millions and millions of Eva Smiths and John Smiths still left with us, with their lives, their hopes and fears, their suffering and chance of happiness, all intertwined with our lives, and what we think and say and do. We don't live alone. We are members of one body. We are responsible for each other. And I tell you that the time will soon come when, if men will not learn that lesson, then they will be taught it in fire and blood and anguish. Good night.

He walks straight out, leaving them staring, subdued and wondering.

ACTIVITY 6

1 Compare how the working classes are shown being exploited by their employers in the two extracts. How do the employers justify or maintain their positions? The political message extends beyond the workers in the factories in both extracts. How do the writers do this?

2 How do the two writers convey their points of view? Think about the structure of the extract from *Hard Times*, in which the description of Coketown adds to the oppressive effect, and the use of syntax and irony convey the deadening effect of the town on its people. In the extract from *An Inspector Calls* you could think about the ways Priestley uses the exchanges between characters, the interventions of other characters, the language of the Inspector at the end, and his exit to achieve effects. After

considering their points of view, compare how the writers use different forms to the same purpose.

3   *Hard Times* was written in 1854, and *An Inspector Calls* in 1945, though it was set in 1912. Which of these are significant contexts, in your view? Think about events going on and the state of society during these years.

4   Now write a comparison of the extracts.

A psychoanalytic reading of the nature of obsession in the novel *Enduring Love* by Ian McEwan and in either *Hamlet* or *Othello* by William Shakespeare would provide some illuminating connections and comparisons. *King Lear* is also open to a Marxist interpretation, but comparing it with Thomas Hardy's *Far From the Madding Crowd* would raise issues of family and power, gender and power, and nature and man as well.

Assessment Objective 5ii

> evaluate the significance of cultural, historical and other contextual influences on literary texts and study

AO5ii is not tested as such in this module, but AO2 'respond with knowledge and understanding to literary texts of different types and periods' is, and considering different contexts is a fruitful way of comparing texts. Examples are given below of a number of broad contextual areas for you to consider, with texts used to illustrate them.

Historical context

Many texts have a historical context which is significant for the reader. In pairing texts, the contexts themselves might be comparable, or the ways the writers use the contexts might be similar. For instance, Peter Ackroyd in *Hawksmoor* and Barry Unsworth in *Sacred Hunger* both write about eighteenth-century society, but use that context in very different ways. Read the extracts from these two twentieth-century novels below, and work through the questions that follow in Activity 7.

In this extract from *Sacred Hunger*, Paris is remembering his confinement in Norwich Jail:

In prison I was subject also to defect of heat, he thought, remembering the stone floor, the bare walls. At this interval of time Norwich Jail had assumed the shape of a pit in his mind, with descending levels of damnation. At the lowest level were those who had no money at all and small means of obtaining any. He had been one week here, on the orders of the outraged cleric who owned the prison, as punishment for printing seditious views concerning God's creation. Here men and women fought with rats in damp cellars for scraps of food thrown down to them through a trap-door, and huddled together for warmth upon heaps of filthy rags and bundles of rotten straw. Lunatics stumbled about here, women gave birth, people died of fever or starvation.

These were people yielding no profit. Higher in the scale were those who could pay for food and a private room and it was here that Paris, until redeemed by his uncle, had found lodging. Two shillings a week had provided him also with writing materials and given him access to the prisoners' common-room, where there were newspapers, and a fire in the coldest weather; but it had not been enough to free him from the stench of the place, nor the brutalities of some of his fellow-inmates – thieves and pimps mingled with debtors here. Higher yet, serenely above all this and freed from unpleasant associations, were the rich prisoners, who lived as the bishop's guests and entertained on a lavish scale.

Norwich Jail had given Paris his notion of hell, and its workings afforded an example of docility to law every bit as absolute as the motions of the blood postulated by Harvey. Money regulated every smallest detail of the place, from the paupers in the cellars to the profligate feasters above. All rents went to the bishop, who had spent a thousand pounds to acquire the prison and was laudably set on making his investment as profitable as possible, this being a time when the individual pursuit of wealth was regarded as inherently virtuous, on the grounds that it increased the wealth and well-being of the community. Indeed, this process of enrichment was generally referred to as 'wealth-creation' by the theorists of the day. The spread of benefits was not apparent in the prison itself, owing to the special circumstances there and particularly to the very high death-rate.

The keepers at their lower level sought to emulate the governor, pursuing wealth diligently through the sale of spirits, the purveying of harlots and the extortionate charges to visitors.

In this extract from *Hawksmoor*, the narrator, the architect Nicholas Dyer, is visiting a lunatic asylum with Sir Christopher Wren:

[. . .] since there is nothing finer in an idle Hour than to make merry among the Lunaticks, I agreed to take that Course and walk with him that Way. We were admitted thro' the iron Gate of Bedlam and, having given Sixpence, turned in thro' another Barricado into the Gallery of the Men's Apartments where there was such a rattling of Chains and drumming of Doors that it made a body's Head ache. The Noise and Roaring, the Swearing and Clamour, the Stench and Nastinesse, and all the Croud of afflicted Things to be seen there, joyn'd together to make the Place seem a very Emblem of Hell and a kind of Entrance into it.

We walked through with Linnen pressed against our Nostrils, and Sir Chris. gave his bright Glances all around at this assembly of derang'd Creatures. Some of the Mad who peeped through their Wickets were indeed known to him, for he had set them down in his Pocket-book before, and when one magoty-brained Fellow called out *Masters, Masters!* Sir Chris. murmured to me, Do not turn back but go on a little and see the Conclusion to his Cries. For there were others who, on hearing him, went back to hear what he had to say and, when they came close to his Wicket, he provided them all with a plentifull Bowl of Piss which he cast very successfully amongst them, singing out: I never give Victuals but I give Drink and you're welcome, Gentlemen. He is a merry Fellow, *said Sir Chris.* with a laugh. Then as we passed down this Passage we were knocked against certain Women of the Town, who gave us Eye-language, since there were many Corners and Closets in Bedlam where they would stop and wait for Custom: indeed it was known as a sure Market for Lechers and Loiterers, for tho' they came in Single they went out by Pairs. This is a Showing-room for Whores, *I said.*

And what better place for Lust, *Sir. Chris. replied,* than among those whose Wits have fled?

ACTIVITY 7

1 List the similarities in the description of physical conditions in the two institutions.

2 What do you observe about the administration of the two institutions, in terms of the principles governing them?

3 What are the attitudes to money and women in the two institutions? Which seems more important to each writer?

4 There are many references to hell in both extracts, but these are more noticeable in *Sacred Hunger*. Pick out the references and compare each writer's use of hell as a metaphor.

5 What are the attitudes of Paris and Dyer to the conditions they see? How are they similar, and how are they different? How are their attitudes conveyed?

If you were answering a question on these two texts as a pair, you would need to look at the wider picture each novel offers of the period, and the way each text uses a second narrative at different time periods. Language would also be a focal point of comparison.

Social context

Many writers use their work to comment on the social context in which their text is set. Dickens is an obvious example, and his descriptions of Coketown in *Hard Times* or London in *Bleak House* could be compared and contrasted with William Blake's treatment of urban life in his poetry. This could be expanded, too, into an examination of form and language.

Many writers also comment on their own society by setting their texts in other societies. Brian Friel's play *Translations*, for instance, is set in 1833, but at its first performance in Derry in 1980 the issues raised by the presence of English soldiers would have been very relevant to the lives of the audience.

Two writers who reflected on developments in their societies in the 1930s and 1940s were Aldous Huxley in *Brave New World*, and George Orwell in *1984*. At this time people were beginning to realise the potential power of the mass media. Read these passages, and answer the questions that follow in Activity 8.

In these excerpts from the first chapter of *1984*, Winston is attending the Two Minutes Hate. The film they are watching shows Emmanuel Goldstein, the enemy of Oceania (Winston's country):

The next moment a hideous, grinding speech, as of some monstrous machine running without oil, burst from the big telescreen at the end of the room. It was a noise that set one's teeth on edge and bristled the hair at the back of one's neck. The Hate had started. [. . .]

Before the Hate had proceeded for thirty seconds, uncontrollable exclamations of rage were breaking out from half the people in the room. The self-satisfied sheeplike face on the screen, and the terrifying power of the Eurasian army behind it, were too much to be borne: besides, the sight or even the thought of Goldstein produced fear and anger automatically. [. . .]

In its second minute the Hate rose to a frenzy. People were leaping up and down in their places and shouting at the tops of their voices in an effort to drown the maddening bleating voice that came from the screen. The little sandy-haired woman had turned bright pink, and her mouth was opening and shutting like that of a landed fish. Even O'Brien's heavy face was flushed. He was sitting very straight in his chair, his powerful chest swelling and quivering as though he were standing up to the assault of a wave. The dark-haired girl behind Winston had begun crying out 'Swine! Swine! Swine!' and suddenly she picked up a heavy Newspeak dictionary and flung it at the screen. It struck Goldstein's nose and bounced off; the voice continued inexorably. In a lucid moment Winston found that he was shouting with the others and kicking his heel violently against the rung of his chair. The horrible thing about the Two Minutes Hate was not that one was obliged to act a part, but, on the contrary, that it was impossible to avoid joining in. Within thirty seconds any pretence was always unnecessary. A hideous ecstasy of fear and vindictiveness, a desire to kill, to torture, to smash faces in with a sledge hammer, seemed to flow through the whole group of people like an electric current, turning one even against one's will into a grimacing, screaming lunatic.

Brave New World by Aldous Huxley is set in a future society where World Controllers have created an ideal society through genetic science, where pleasure and promiscuity are compulsory, and solitude and romance discouraged. In these excerpts from Chapter XI, Lenina and a man raised outside this society, known as the Savage, go to the 'feelies':

'Take hold of those metal knobs on the arms of your chair,' whispered Lenina. 'Otherwise you won't get any of the feely effects.'

The Savage did as he was told.

[. . .] there were ten seconds of complete darkness; then suddenly, dazzling and incomparably more solid-looking than they would have seemed in actual flesh and blood, far more real than reality, there stood the stereoscopic images, locked in one another's arms, of a gigantic Negro and a golden-haired brachycephalic Beta-Plus female.

The Savage started. That sensation on his lips! He lifted a hand to his mouth; the titillation ceased; let his hand fall back on the metal knob; it began again. The scent organ, meanwhile, breathed pure musk. Expiringly, a sound-track super-dove cooed 'Oo-ooh'; and vibrating only thirty-two times a second, a deeper than African bass made an answer: 'Aa-aah.' 'Ooh-ah! Ooh-ah!' the stereoscopic lips came together again, and once more the facial erogenous zones of the six thousand spectators in the Alhambra tingled with almost intolerable galvanic pleasure. 'Ooh . . .'

The plot of the film was extremely simple. A few minutes after the first Ooh's and Aah's (a duet having been sung and a little love made on that famous bearskin, every hair of which – the Assistant Predestinator was perfectly right – could be separately and distinctly felt), the Negro had a helicopter accident, fell on his head. Thump! what a twinge through the forehead! A chorus of *ow's* and *aie's* went up from the audience. [. . .]

Then the bearskin made a final appearance and, amid a blare of sexophones, the last stereoscopic kiss faded into darkness, the last electric titillation died on the lips like a dying moth that quivers, quivers ever more feebly, ever more faintly, and at last is quite, quite still.

But for Lenina the moth did not completely die. Even after the lights had gone up, while they were shuffling slowly along with the crowd towards the lifts, its ghost still fluttered against her lips, still traced fine shuddering roads of anxiety and pleasure across her skin. Her cheeks were flushed, her eyes dewily bright, her breath came deeply. She caught hold of the Savage's arm and pressed it, limp, against her side. Her looked down at her for a moment, pale, pained, desiring, and ashamed of his desire.

ACTIVITY 8

Answer the following questions in note form to begin with. Then write a full comparison of the two passages.

1 Compare the physical effects of the films on the audience in each text.

2 Compare the emotional effects of the films on the audience in each text.

3 In the *1984* extract, the thought of Goldstein 'produced fear and anger automatically'. Find evidence of other 'automatic' responses in both passages.

4 Look carefully at the relationship between what is seen and felt from the films, and the responses produced. Notice, too, the responses which are presented by the writer as individual, and those which are mass responses – that the whole audience has at the same time.

5 Although both writers show audiences responding in the same way, in each text there are hints that one character does not share the mass feeling, or at least has mixed feelings. Look for evidence of this in each text.

6 The responses of the characters to the films are clearly of a different nature in the two texts. How do you think this might reflect the nature of the societies presented by the writers?

7 The tones of the two texts are also very different. How are the tones established? Does either of the passages use humour? Finally, consider how the tone of each passage could tell you something about the writers' intentions.

There are many socio-cultural areas which might also allow for interesting and illuminating comparisons. *Trainspotting* by Irving Welsh and the play *Shopping and Fucking* by Mark Ravenshill, for instance, both deal with drug culture, and you could make comparisons of language and structure. The novel *The French Lieutenant's Woman* by John Fowles and the play *Mrs Warren's Profession* by George Bernard Shaw both revolve around issues of love, marriage and prostitution, but make very different cultural assumptions. As well as the difference in form, one is a chronological narrative and one non-chronological, offering further scope for contrast. A comparison of *Oranges Are Not the Only Fruit* by Jeanette Winterson with *Wild Swans* by Jung Chang would offer, in two very different narratives, perspectives on growing up in restrictive cultures.

A particular socio-economic concept, which forms a context for many American texts, is the 'American Dream' – the idea that working to acquire money and material goods will bring success, and with it every kind of happiness. Two texts which both reflect on this are *The Great Gatsby* by Scott Fitzgerald and the play *Death of a Salesman* by Arthur Miller: extracts from both are given below.

In this extract from *The Great Gatsby*, the narrator, Nick, is describing the parties at the house of his new neighbour, Jay Gatsby:

At least once a fortnight a corps of caterers came down with several hundred feet of canvas and enough coloured lights to make a Christmas tree of Gatsby's enormous garden. On buffet tables, garnished with glistening hors-d'œuvre, spiced baked hams crowded against salads of harlequin designs and pastry pigs and turkeys bewitched to a dark gold. In the main hall a bar with a real brass rail was set up, and stocked with gins and liquors and with cordials so long forgotten that most of his female guests were too young to know one from another.

By seven o'clock the orchestra has arrived, no thin five-piece affair, but a whole pitful of oboes and trombones and saxophones and viols and cornets and piccolos, and low and high drums. The last swimmers have come in from the beach now and are dressing upstairs; the cars from New York are parked five deep in the drive, and already the halls and salons and verandas are gaudy with primary colours, and hair bobbed in strange new ways, and shawls beyond the dreams of Castile. The bar is in full swing, and floating rounds of cocktails permeate the garden outside, until the air is alive with chatter and laughter, and casual innuendo and introductions forgotten on the spot, and enthusiastic meetings between women who never knew each other's names.

The lights grow brighter as the earth lurches away from the sun, and now the orchestra is playing yellow cocktail music, and the opera of voices pitches a key higher. Laughter is easier minute by minute, spilled with prodigality, tipped out at a cheerful word. The groups change more swiftly, swell with new arrivals, dissolve and form in the same breath; already there are wanderers, confident girls who weave here and there among the stouter and more stable, become for a sharp, joyous moment the centre of a group, and then, excited with triumph, glide on through the sea-change of faces and voices and colour under the constantly changing light.

Suddenly one of these gypsies, in trembling opal, seizes a cocktail out of the air, dumps it down for courage and, moving her hands like Frisco, dances out alone on the canvas platform. A momentary hush; the orchestra leader varies his rhythm obligingly for her, and there is a burst of chatter as the erroneous news goes around that she is Gilda Gray's understudy from the *Follies*. The party has begun.

This scene from Miller's *Death of a Salesman* shows Willy Loman contemplating killing himself so that his family can get the insurance money. Willy, a salesman, is ill, and has been fired from his job. He feels guilty about his lack of success, the trouble his wife has had to endure, and the contempt that his son Biff feels for him. Here he is 'talking' to his Uncle Ben, who was a successful entrepreneur; the conversation takes place in Willy's imagination:

WILLY	[. . .] What a proposition, ts, ts. Terrific, terrific. 'Cause she's suffered, Ben, the woman has suffered. You understand me? A man can't go out the way he came in, Ben, a man has got to add up to something. You can't, you can't – [*Ben moves towards him as though to interrupt.*] You gotta consider, now. Don't answer so quick. Remember, it's a guaranteed twenty-thousand-dollar proposition. Now look, Ben, I want you to go through the ins and outs of this thing with me. I've got nobody to talk to, Ben, and the woman has suffered, you hear me?
BEN	[*standing still, considering*] What's the proposition?
WILLY	It's twenty thousand dollars on the barrelhead. Guaranteed, gilt-edged, you understand?
BEN	You don't want to make a fool of yourself. They might not honour the policy.
WILLY	How can they dare refuse? Didn't I work like a coolie to meet every premium on the nose? And now they don't pay off! Impossible!
BEN	It's called a cowardly thing, William.
WILLY	Why? Does it take more guts to stand here the rest of my life ringing up a zero?
BEN	[*yielding*] That's a point, William. [*He moves, thinking, turns.*] And twenty thousand – that *is* something one can feel with the hand, it is there.
WILLY	[*now assured, with rising power*] Oh, Ben, that's the whole beauty of it! I see it like a diamond, shining in the dark, hard and rough, that I can pick up and touch in my hand. Not like – like an appointment! This would not be another damned-fool appointment, Ben, and it changes all the aspects. Because he thinks I'm nothing, see, and so he spites me. But the funeral – [*straightening up*] Ben, that funeral will be massive! They'll come from Maine, Massachusetts, Vermont, New Hampshire! All the old-timers with the strange licence plates – that boy will be thunderstruck, Ben, because he never realized – I am known! Rhode Island, New York, New Jersey – I am known, Ben, and he'll see it with his eyes once and for all. He'll see what I am, Ben! He's in for a shock, that boy!
BEN	[*coming down to the edge of the garden*] He'll call you a coward.
WILLY	[*suddenly fearful*] No, that would be terrible.
BEN	Yes. And a damned fool.
WILLY	No, no, he mustn't, I won't have that! [*He is broken and desperate.*]
BEN	He'll hate you, William.

ACTIVITY 9

1 In the extract from *The Great Gatsby*, look for the words and phrases in which suggest:

- abundance, and excess

- a dream-like, or unreal quality

- a transitory feeling

- that things are false – although an effect has been aimed for, it doesn't quite succeed.

2 In the extract from *Death of a Salesman*, look for evidence in Willy's language of his desire to succeed. What else seems to drive him?

3 Willy is planning to kill himself, but he describes it like a business deal. Look for evidence of this in the extract.

4 Find examples of Willy's sense of his own failure.

5 Willy has always deluded himself about his own achievements. Can you find allusions to this in the passage?

6 The extract from *The Great Gatsby* comes early on in the novel (Chapter 2) but both texts end in the failure and death of the central figures. Using all the evidence you've accumulated, show how both extracts present the American Dream as a false, dangerous concept.

Language context

All literary texts have a language context, but in some language is a pronounced feature. Brian Friel's play *Translations*, and George Orwell's novel *1984* both deal with the power of language to affect society and the individual. Read these two extracts and work through Activity 10 below.

In this extract from *1984* the central character, Winston Smith, is listening to a colleague in the Ministry of Truth telling him about the advantages of Newspeak. Newspeak is the language of Big Brother, who is the figurehead of the totalitarian state in which the novel is set.

'[. . .] Do you know that Newspeak is the only language in the world whose vocabulary gets smaller every year?'

Winston did know that, of course. He smiled, sympathetically he hoped, not trusting himself to speak. Syme bit off another fragment of the dark-coloured bread, chewed it briefly, and went on:

'Don't you see that the whole aim of Newspeak is to narrow the range of thought? In the end we shall make thoughtcrime literally impossible, because there will be no words in which to express it. Every concept that can ever be needed will be expressed by exactly *one* word, with its meaning rigidly defined and all its subsidiary meanings rubbed out and forgotten. Already, in the Eleventh Edition, we're not far from that point. But the process will still be continuing long after you and I are dead. Every year fewer and fewer words, and the range of consciousness always a little smaller. Even now, of course, there's no reason or excuse for committing thoughtcrime. It's merely a question of self-discipline, reality-control. But in the end there won't be any need even for that. The Revolution will be complete when the language is perfect. Newspeak is Ingsoc and Ingsoc is Newspeak,' he added with a sort of mystical satisfaction. 'Has it ever occurred to you, Winston, that by the year 2050, at the very latest, not a single human being will be alive who could understand such a conversation as we are having now?'

'Except – ' began Winston doubtfully, and then stopped.

It had been on the tip of his tongue to say 'Except the proles,' but he checked himself, not feeling fully certain that this remark was not in some way unorthodox.

In this extract from Brian Friel's play *Translations*, Lancey, an English soldier, is warning the villagers of Ballybeg what will happen if his fellow officer, who has gone missing, is not found. In the play, set in the west of Ireland in 1833, Owen has been translating the officers' words into Irish, and has been helping to give English names to Irish places. Sarah, who was mute at the beginning of the play, has learned to speak during the course of the play.

LANCEY	If that doesn't bear results, commencing forty-eight hours from now we will embark on a series of evictions and levelling of every abode in the following selected areas –
OWEN	You're not – !
LANCEY	Do your job. Translate.
OWEN	If they still haven't found him in two days' time they'll begin evicting and levelling every house starting with these townlands.
	[*Lancey reads from his list.*]
LANCEY	Swinefort.
OWEN	Lis na Muc.
LANCEY	Burnfoot.
OWEN	Bun na hAbhann.
LANCEY	Dromduff.
OWEN	Druim Dubh.
LANCEY	Whiteplains.

OWEN	Machaire Ban.
LANCEY	Kings Head.
OWEN	Cnoc na Ri.
LANCEY	If by then the lieutenant hasn't been found, we will proceed until a complete clearance is made of this entire section.
OWEN	If Yolland hasn't been got by then, they will ravish the whole parish.
LANCEY	I trust they know exactly what they've got to do.

[*Pointing to Bridget*] I know you. I know where you live.

[*Pointing to Sarah*] Who are you? Name!

[*Sarah's mouth opens and shuts, opens and shuts. Her face becomes contorted.*]

What's your name?

[*Again Sarah tries frantically.*]

OWEN	Go on, Sarah. You can tell him.

[*But Sarah cannot. And she knows she cannot. She closes her mouth. Her head goes down.*]

OWEN	Her name is Sarah Johnny Sally.
LANCEY	Where does she live?
OWEN	Bun na hAbhann.
LANCEY	Where?
OWEN	Burnfoot.

ACTIVITY 10

1   Describe how language, and rules about language, are used to oppress people in the societies of each extract? Be as detailed and exact as you can.

2   *1984* is set in a society in the future, and *Translations* is set in a society in the past. What does each writer seem to be suggesting about the society they present?

3   In each extract one character does not speak, although Winston starts to and stops in *1984*. What might their silence suggest to the reader of *1984*, and the audience of *Translations*? Look at the stage directions, and work out how the play operates in a different way from the novel.

If you were comparing these two texts, you could go on to look at the importance of language in the whole texts. These two extracts would be good starting points.

Invented language is a feature of some texts, and could be an important element in comparing, say, *1984* with *A Clockwork Orange* by Anthony Burgess.

Literary and generic context

Comparing two texts by the same writer involves a literary context, that of the writer's work. Other contexts, such as period, will be involved too, and style and subject matter can also be compared. There are likely to be similarities, of course, but there may also be significant differences. The writer's intentions in the texts may be quite different, a range of conventions could be used, and the works may represent different stages in the writer's development.

Below are the openings to two novels by Jane Austen, *Pride and Prejudice* and *Mansfield Park*. Read these extracts, and work through Activity 11 below.

It is a truth universally acknowledged, that a single man in possession of a good fortune must be in want of a wife.

However little known the feelings or views of such a man may be on his first entering a neighbourhood, this truth is so well fixed in the minds of the surrounding families, that he is considered as the rightful property of someone or other of their daughters.

'My dear Mr Bennet,' said his lady to him one day, 'have you heard that Netherfield Park is let at last?'

Mr Bennet replied that he had not.

'But it is,' returned she; 'for Mrs Long has just been here, and she told me all about it.'

Mr Bennet made no answer.

'Do not you want to know who has taken it?' cried his wife impatiently.

'*You* want to tell me, and I have no objection to hearing it.'

This was invitation enough.

'Why, my dear, you must know, Mrs Long says that Netherfield is taken by a young man of large fortune from the north of England; that he came down on Monday in a chaise and four to see the place, and was so much delighted with it, that he agreed with Mr Morris immediately; that he is to take possession before Michaelmas, and some of his servants are to be in the house by the end of next week.'

'What is his name?'

'Bingley.'

'Is he married or single?'

'Oh! single, my dear, to be sure! A single man of large fortune; four or five thousand a year. What a fine thing for our girls!'

'How so? How can it affect them?'

'My dear Mr Bennet,' replied his wife, 'how can you be so tiresome! You must know that I am thinking of his marrying one of them.'

'Is that his design in settling here?'

'Design! Nonsense, how can you talk so! But it is very likely that he *may* fall in love with one of them, and therefore you must visit him as soon as he comes.'

'I see no occasion for that. You and the girls may go, or you may send them by themselves, which perhaps will be still better, for as you are as handsome as any of them, Mr Bingley might like you the best of the party.'

(J. Austen, *Pride and Prejudice*)

About thirty years ago, Miss Maria Ward, of Huntingdon, with only seven thousand pounds, had the good luck to captivate Sir Thomas Bertram, of Mansfield Park, in the county of Northampton, and to be thereby raised to the rank of a baronet's lady, with all the comforts and consequences of an handsome house and large income. All Huntingdon exclaimed on the greatness of the match, and her uncle, the lawyer, himself allowed her to be at least three thousand pounds short of any equitable claim to it. She had two sisters to be benefited by her elevation; and such of their acquaintances as thought Miss Ward and Miss Frances quite as handsome as Miss Maria, did not scruple to predict their marrying with almost equal advantage. But there certainly are not so many men of large fortune in the world as there are pretty women to deserve them. Miss Ward, at the end of half-a-dozen years, found herself obliged to be attached to the Rev. Mr Norris, a friend of her brother-in-law, with scarcely any private fortune, and Miss Frances fared yet worse. Miss Ward's match, indeed, when it came to the point, was not contemptible; Sir Thomas being happily able to give his friend an income in the living of Mansfield; and Mr and Mrs Norris began their career of conjugal felicity with very little less than a thousand a year. But Miss Frances married, in the common phrase, to disoblige her family, and by fixing on a lieutenant of marines, without education, fortune, or connections, did it very thoroughly. She could hardly have made a more untoward choice. Sir Thomas Bertram had interest which, from principle as well as pride – from a general wish of doing right, and a desire of seeing all that were connected with him in situations of respectability, he would have been glad to exert for the advantage of Lady Bertram's sister; but her husband's profession was such as no interest could reach; and before he had time to devise any other method of assisting them, an absolute breach between the sisters had taken place. It was the natural result of the conduct of each party, and such as a very imprudent marriage almost always produces.

(J. Austen, *Mansfield Park*)

ACTIVITY 11

1 Referring to both extracts, what does Jane Austen suggest is the most important element in making a marriage? What is unimportant? How are these things conveyed? Look for all the references to money, and notice which extract has the most references.

2 Find examples of humour in the extracts. Which extract has more humour? Notice whether the humour relies on language or character.

3 Look for the abstract nouns in each extract. Which extract has more? Do you see any condemnation in either extract?

4 Although the language in both extracts is naturally fairly similar, the form is used differently. Look at the way the two extracts are set out on the page and note the main differences. How is character conveyed in each extract?

5 Having worked through the questions above, try to sum up the differences in tone and intention of the two extracts.

If you were answering a question on these two texts, you could look at how marriage is viewed in each novel as a whole, and at the differences in tone.

Another type of literary context occurs when one text refers to another. This is the case with Charlotte Brontë's *Jane Eyre* and *Wide Sargasso Sea* by Jean Rhys, in which Rhys explores a character from Brontë's (earlier) novel; or *Precious Bane* by Mary Webb and *Cold Comfort Farm* by Stella Gibbons. Gibbons's novel is a parody of the rural genre to which *Precious Bane* belonged.

Developments in literary forms and conventions can also form a context, and comparisons between texts can illuminate the issues. In first-person narratives, for instance, the narrator might be 'reliable' or 'unreliable'. The effect on the reader of the 'unreliable' narrator in *The Remains of the Day* by Kazuo Ishiguro, for example, could be examined by comparing it with the effect of the narrative in *David Copperfield*, by Charles Dickens. On the other hand, comparing it with a similar narrative of self-delusion in Dickens's *Great Expectations* would also be interesting.

Texts within particular literary genres could be compared, too. In detective fiction, *The Lady in the Lake* by Raymond Chandler could be compared with any of the 'Aurelio Zen' novels by Michael Dibdin, or either of these could be compared with Ian McEwan's *Enduring Love*, which has strong elements of thriller writing, though used here for different purposes. Gothic or horror novels from different periods could also be compared.

Coursework

If you choose to enter for the coursework unit, you will have to study and compare at least two texts, one of which must be a prose text, and produce an essay of about 2,500 words in length. You can write the essays in school or at college or at home, and then they will be marked by your teacher. Finally, the moderator from the Examination Board will look at your work and all the work from your school or centre, and decide on a final mark. In order to do well in your coursework, you need to think about these points:

- choosing a task
- reading the text
- planning
- research
- writing
- drafting and redrafting
- sticking to word and time limits.

Choosing a task

It is vital to choose a task which is appropriate – a task that addresses the Assessment Objectives. This module represents 15% of the whole A Level examination, and 30% of A2. It assesses equally Assessment Objectives 1, 3 and 4, with special emphasis on AO2ii (this accounts for nearly half of the marks available). This means that you must choose a task which is not simply about two texts, but which offers good opportunities for a thorough comparison. You must choose a task which enables you to address writers' choices of form, language and structure, too, and one which leads you to an independent judgement. It is easy to get very involved in comparing subject matter and to forget that you have to do more than this. Your task needs to be achievable, as well: if you're setting out to write a 2,500-word piece, there's no point in setting yourself a task which can't be done in less than 10,000 words. Word limits are very important. As a general rule, the more sharply defined the task is, the better.

Reading the text

You'll probably read the texts in class, at least partially, where you'll have the chance to discuss them with your teacher and other students. But just like your exam texts for Module 4, you'll need to read them again yourself too. You need to show 'knowledge and understanding' of the texts (AO2ii) in your writing, and the more you read them the better your chances of finding and exploring connections and comparisons between them. This will enable you to draw on a wide range of evidence when you write your final essay.

Planning

Now you need to plan your essay. Here are three general points to bear in mind.

1 Your plan needs to be helpful to you in writing your essay, so that in working through it, you produce a logical sequence of ideas, which develop an argument and lead to a clear conclusion.

2 You need to check your plan against the Assessment Objectives. Is it clear how and at what point you're going to meet them?

3 You don't want to have to change your plan much once you've started writing, so think about length again at this stage. By the time your plan is fleshed out with argument and evidence, will the word count be about right? Too many words? Too few to create a solid argument? If it doesn't look right, change your plan now.

Research

Research may well involve reading articles or essays about your texts, from books or the internet, but the most important source of information is still the primary source – the texts themselves. For instance, if you decided to write about the ways the American Dream is presented in *The Great Gatsby* and *Death of a Salesman*, you'd begin with a selective re-reading of the texts, looking for ideas and passages which might be useful to you. You could then research the writers, or the concept of the American Dream, to see if you could add to the ideas you already have, or to find some new angles to develop, or to provide additional evidence. If you have read secondary sources as part of your research, you must mention them in the bibliography at the end of your essay.

Writing

A significant proportion of the marks available for this module are for writing, and in coursework you have the chance to score well – perhaps more easily than you can in timed examinations. Five of the thirty marks are for the ability to 'communicate clearly the knowledge, understanding and insight appropriate to literary study, using appropriate terminology and accurate and coherent written expression' (AO1). As long as you give yourself plenty of time to write, you can take more care over the accuracy and clarity of your coursework essay than you can in an examination – and you can take the time to check it, revise it and improve it when you've finished the first draft. There are specific marks for this, so do take the trouble to collect them.

Assessment Objective 2ii is the dominant Objective here. After all, this module is about 'literary connections', and the second part of this Objective asks you to explore and comment on 'relationships and comparisons between literary texts'. You still have to meet the first part of the Objective, though, and show your ability to 'respond with knowledge and understanding to a literary text'. Your understanding will be demonstrated in the quality of your argument; but knowledge has to underpin everything you write, in an examination or in coursework. In coursework you have the leisure to practise what you have to do under time pressure in the examinations – to provide evidence for what you say from the text. There are appropriate ways of showing knowledge, too. You can show it by referring to details or echoes of the text, or by quotation. Short quotations (usually the most effective) can be included in the body of your writing, while longer quotations can be written on separate lines, so that they are easier to read. If you're quoting lines of verse in the body of your writing, you should show the line divisions.

If you are quoting from a secondary source, such as a critic, this should be footnoted, by numbering the quotations and providing a guide to the numbers, either at the foot of the page or at the end of the essay. Here is an example:

'Bernard is, in fact, living proof that the system's effectiveness, an affirmation of the proposition that persistent application of one's talents, small though they may be, pays off. And this, after all, is the substance of the American Dream'[1]

The note at the bottom of the page or the end of the essay would be:

1 Gardner, R. H.: p. 65 'Tragedy of the Lowest Man' from Splintered Stage (1965).

If you do use the words of other writers such as critics in your own writing, you must acknowledge them. You have to sign a declaration that the coursework is your own work, and if you 'lift' from other writing without acknowledging it, it is called malpractice, and you could lose all your marks for the module.

Drafting and redrafting

When you have completed a first draft of your coursework essay, your teacher may allow you to redraft it, as long as there is enough time left to do so. Your teacher is only allowed to give general advice and guidelines as to how you might improve the work, *not* to correct it and rewrite it – the coursework essay must be your work, after all. Of course, you should heed any advice, but you should try and make your first draft as good as you can. It's a lot easier to make minor changes than major ones at this stage.

Sticking to word and time limits

The word limit for A2 coursework is 2,500 words. If you exceed it, you will run the risk of being penalised. If your first draft comes to 3,000 words, you can probably trim it fairly easily, and you can ask for your teacher's guidance as to which parts to prune. If it is 5,000 words, though, you may have problems. Cutting sentences here and there, and tightening expression, won't cut it by half. It is likely in that situation, that you made a mistake early on – either in selecting the task, at the planning stage, or when you were partway through. If it looks as if you will run over the word limit, you should stop and review your work as soon as possible. Your teacher will give you the coursework deadlines, and it is important to stick to them – not just to please your teacher, but to improve your chances of success. You will only be able to cut/redraft/rethink if you've got the time to do it.

Planning coursework: some strategies

The first part of Module 5, Literary Connections, was designed to offer you a range of methods for comparing texts, and at the same time a choice of possible combinations of texts. Once you've chosen and read texts, and decided on and discussed a task with your teacher (who has to get the agreement of the coursework moderator), then it's time to start planning. Below are some strategies you could adopt and the principles outlined will apply to any choice of texts. The plans are based on the study of *Birdsong* by Sebastian Faulks and the war poetry of Wilfred Owen, which were looked at at the beginning of the module. The task is: 'An exploration of the ways war is presented in *Birdsong* and Wilfred Owen's poetry'. Methods 1 and 2 involve looking first at one text, then the other.

Methods 1 and 2 involve looking first at one text, then the other.

Methods 3 and 4 involve looking at the two texts *alongside* each other. If you organise your work by looking at the two texts like this, 'systematic comparisons', and 'developing ideas by comparison and contrast' should both be possible. There are a number of ways of doing this; Methods 3 and 4 are just two examples.

Method 1

The simplest way to start is to deal with one text, then the other, then draw together comparisons and contrasts. However, this is unlikely to be the most effective method to choose. The teachers and moderators who assess your work do not favour one method over another, but they do mark against the Assessment Criteria. The criteria for the top two bands for AO2ii for this module are:

- systematic comparisons of form, structure and language as well as subject and theme (Band 3 11–15)

- skilfully selects for analysis specific aspects of texts, clarifying and developing ideas by comparison and contrast (Band 4 16–20).

As you can see, 'systematic comparisons' and 'developing ideas by comparison and contrast' will be difficult to achieve with this method, especially within 2,500 words. A method which produces sharper focus will be more likely to score really well.

Method 2

A similar method would be to write about one text, and then to compare and contrast elements as you write about the second. Looking at the criteria quoted above, this would allow you to make 'systematic comparisons', but 'developing ideas by comparison and contrast' might be a little more difficult. Your thinking and writing about the texts will still have to be very organised, or you will find yourself including material on one of the texts – probably the first – for which there is no relationship in the other text. This material would then be irrelevant to your argument.

Method 3

You could organise your comparison by subject matter. In the case of the task on *Birdsong* and the poetry of Owen, there are elements of war which both writers deal with, so you could make a plan charting a logical sequence of elements, and then write about how the writers present these elements. It might look something like this:

1 Introduction.

2 Trench conditions – mud, cold, disease, effects of noise, madness.

3 Wounds – including self-inflicted.

4 Death – types of death inc. gas, mines, tunnelling, death of the young.

5 Attitudes to officers and generals.

6 Attitudes to the enemy.

7 Conclusion, linking writers' tones and intentions.

This would work well enough, and should allow you to develop and explore ideas about relationships and comparisons which remain relevant. A danger here would be over-enthusiasm for the subject matter, to the exclusion of style. Remember, you have to address AO3, and the question asked 'how the writers present' – an invitation to write about 'how writers' choices of form, structure and language shape meanings'.

Method 4

You could organise your comparison by style instead of subject matter, by working through a comparison of the ways the writers choose form, structure and language to shape meanings. You can't overlook AO3 if you do this, and the subject matter should be easier to deal with. A plan might look like this:

1 *Introduction* You could begin by comparing the two extracts about shell-holes from the two texts given on pages 88–9 of this book. This would both illustrate some commonality of subject, and lead you into a discussion of form.

2 *Form* You could pick up from the extracts Faulks's use of dialogue, although Owen uses dialogue too ('The Chances', for instance, is entirely in dialogue, and several other poems make use of speech). *Birdsong* makes use of letters, a form which is not really available to Owen, though 'S.I.W.' contains a fragment of a letter. Owen's distinctive poetic style and use of half-rhyme, however, highlights a genre difference.

3 *Structure* The structures used by the writers are mostly very different, which is a reflection of genre as much as anything. The complex narrative structure of *Birdsong*, with its time shifts and perspectives, opens up angles not available to Owen, especially as Faulks has the advantage of writing from a later

period. On the other hand, Owen also uses shifts in time to make his statements. 'Disabled', 'S.I.W.', and 'The Send-Off' could all be looked at her Owen uses some dramatic beginnings and endings in ways that would be very unusual in prose, which tends to be less concentrated and intense. Prose tends to explain, where poetry suggests.

4 *Language* Despite the differences in genres – you might expect to find more striking use of language in the intense nature of poetry – both texts shape meanings with choices of language which are often similar. If you look at Pair 1 on page 90 you will find some evidence for this. Of course, there is also a range of poetic language devices employed by Owen which Faulks does not use.

5 *Conclusion* – attitudes/intentions. Despite the differences which will have emerged during the essay, it's clear that Faulks and Owen, in their individual ways and from their different perspectives, share some attitudes about the war. There is much evidence of this, some of which will already have been used, but in Pair 2 on pages 91–2 the final word about war seems to be common to both. Nevertheless, Owen's intention was more immediate than Faulks's in one sense, as he intended his poetry to speak to people at the time, an option not open to Faulks.

Each of Methods 3 and 4 may still have its pitfalls – Method 4 runs the risk of being too technical, and failing to link subject matter. The best thing to do is to plan according to your texts and task. With any method, it is essential to remember that you must offer your own views about the effectiveness of the texts, or about how they can be read.

How to secure good marks

When you've followed all the advice above about selecting texts and task, and planning and writing your essay, you need to have an idea of how well you're going to score. Your teacher will help you here, but it's worth knowing exactly how teachers and moderators judge your essay.

The dominant Assessment Objective in this module is AO2ii, which states that:

> Candidates should be able to respond with knowledge and understanding to literary texts of different types and periods, exploring and commenting on relationships between literary texts.

There are four mark bands. Here are the criteria in the top band, which offers 16–20 marks:

- sound knowledge and understanding of text
- mature skills of analysis and synthesis
- range of ideas supported by detailed reading
- crucial aspects of a question clearly identified
- developed, sustained discussion
- secure conceptual grasp

- skilfully selects for analysis specific aspects of texts, clarifying and developing ideas by comparison and contrast.

That's what you have to aim for. By contrast, here are the criteria for the bottom band (which offers 0–6 marks), which will tell you what to avoid if you want to move up the bands:

- simple narration, description of plot

- simple assertion

- unsupported unconnected comments

- frequent irrelevance

- unassimilated notes

- comparisons between texts are mainly on their superficial features.

Assessment Objective 2ii counts for nearly half the marks, but that means that the other three Objectives tested here are also very important, taken together:

AO1 Candidates should be able to communicate clearly the knowledge, understanding and insight appropriate to literary study, using appropriate terminology and accurate written expression.

Top band:

- technically accurate, sophisticated style

- a cogent, well-structured argument

- accurate use of an appropriate, extensive critical vocabulary

- a vocabulary that can cope with the needs of analysis and criticism.

Bottom band:

- frequent lapses in spelling, punctuation, grammar, sentence construction

- limited vocabulary hinders expression

- technical terms often misunderstood

- unclear lines of argument and/or poor deployment of knowledge/evidence.

AO3 Candidates should be able to show detailed understanding of the ways in which choices of form, structure and language shape meanings.

Top band:

- mature and sophisticated analysis of the ways in which different kinds of form, structure and language shape meaning.

Bottom band:

- few (if any) form, structural or language features identified

- very limited (if any) discussion of how language shapes meaning.

AO4   **Candidates should be able to articulate informed independent opinion**
and judgements, showing understanding of different interpretations of
literary texts by different readers.

Top band:

• mature understanding of the significance of differing critical positions
• sophisticated judgement of text based upon an informed consideration of various possibilities.

Bottom band:

• little (if any) understanding of different interpretive approaches
• little personal response based upon slender or misinterpreted evidence or insensitive reading of other opinions or text
• narrow range of meaning asserted.

Examination

If you select the examination unit, you will have to study and compare at least one of the named pairs of texts in the specification. In the examination, you will have to answer one question on one pair of texts in 1 hour 30 minutes. You can take your texts into the examination, and should do so, as the questions are tailored to an open-book examination.

Preparing for the examination

In class, you will no doubt look at various angles of the texts which you are going to write about in the examination, and think about how you might tackle questions. Immediately before the examination, however, you will probably have some time to do the final preparation yourself. What should you do in this time?

The first thing to say is that you should not rely on having your texts with you in the examination to provide information to answer the questions. The texts are simply there for you to use in response to questions which focus on particular passages in the texts. You won't have time to look up other parts of the texts for quotations or information; you need to know all that before you go in.

'Revision' does not just mean looking again at what you've already done. It may be useful to do this when you start to revise, but then you need to re-read as much of your two texts as you can, as close to the examination as you reasonably can, and within a relatively short period of time. The re-reading will refresh information for you, so you have more chance of drawing on it quickly in the exam. You are bound to find new things each time you read a text, and in this case you'll be reading the texts with relationships and comparisons in mind. A plan of action might be:

1   Read over what you've already done – notes, essays, etc.

2   Remind yourself of the sorts of comparisons you might find – reading through the opening pages of the section about Module 5 might be a help.

3 Read the texts, recognising features which fit with the connections you've already recognised, and looking for more.

In the examination – deconstructing the question

When you look at the two questions you have to choose from, and particularly when you have chosen your question, you need to look carefully at the wording to ensure that you know exactly what you have to do – what you have to write about, and how. 'How', of course, will be in line with the Assessment Objectives which you know are being tested. Because they're being tested, they have to be incorporated into the question.

Here are two questions on *Captain Corelli's Mandolin* by Louis de Bernières and *Catch-22* by Joseph Heller:

1 Remind yourself of the episode in *Captain Corelli's Mandolin* which occurs in Chapter 15 'L'Omosessuale' (4) which begins: 'The only things we successfully taught were how to assassinate generals' and ends: '[. . .] could not be more different from the vanished and beloved Francesco, but whom I love as much'.

Also remind yourself of the episode in Chapter 24 of *Catch-22*, 'Milo', from: 'M & M Enterprises verged on collapse' to 'We'll be taking away their incentive'.

Compare and contrast the subject matter and style of these two extracts and consider their importance in the novels.

2 'These novels are very similar: they make you laugh and they make you cry.'

Compare these novels in the light of this remark.

If you choose the first question, the key words to focus on are:

- 'compare and contrast' – which is the dominant Assessment Objective, AO2ii
- 'subject matter' – the first part of AO2ii
- 'style' – AO3
- 'consider' – AO4. You're being asked for your view on their importance
- 'importance' – a reminder that in these extract-based questions you also have to relate these passages to the rest of the text, which is showing both your knowledge and your ability to find relationships within texts.

If you choose the second question, the key words to focus on are:

- 'similar' and 'compare' – again, this refers to the dominant AO2ii
- 'make you' – AO3. This might seem a bit obscure, but you need to look for the invitation to show your knowledge of this aspect of the texts, because AO3 has to be tested. If the novels 'make you' laugh or cry, how have the writers achieved this? What 'choices of form, structure and language' might they have used?
- 'laugh' and 'cry' – invites you to think about subject matter, the things in the novels that might make the reader laugh or cry, and therefore refers to the

first part of AO2 again. It also refers AO4, as it is connected to the reader's response – what is your response to the texts, and to this statement, for each novel?

Planning your response

Sample plans of responses to these two tasks are given below. There are a few important things to remember. First, you must take the time to plan properly. You need to think about the things you want to say, the material to use, and the order to work in. If you are attempting an extract-based question, you may well need to look for the material to use in the extracts as a first step, and these should then be inserted in the right place in your plan. Planning is vital – you need to do it when you're balancing two texts, you've got the time to do it, as you've only got to answer one question in an hour and a half, and planned answers are much more likely to produce high-scoring responses.

Sample questions and plans

The same two questions on the texts *Captain Corelli's Mandolin* and *Catch-22* are repeated below, followed by indications of the elements in the novels you could use in your answers, in a planned sequence. This will give you an idea of the sort of approach you could take on other pairs of texts or similar questions.

> 1 Remind yourself of the episode in *Captain Corelli's Mandolin* which occurs in Chapter 15 'L'Omosessuale' (4) which begins: 'The only things we successfully taught were how to assassinate generals' and ends: '[. . .] could not be more different from the vanished and beloved Francesco, but whom I love as much'. (*Passage A*)
>
> Also remind yourself of the episode in Chapter 24 of *Catch-22*, 'Milo', from: 'M & M Enterprises verged on collapse' to 'We'll be taking away their incentive'. (*Passage B*)
>
> Compare and contrast the subject matter and style of these two extracts and consider their importance in the novels.

In the examination itself the passages you are asked to look at are a little longer than these examples and here only the beginning and the end of the *Catch-22* passage have been provided. The principles of looking at the passages, selecting material, linking to the rest of the novels, and planning are the same.

Passage A

Carlo, an Italian soldier, is describing training Albanian commandos before the death of his friend Francesco.

The only things we successfully taught were how to assassinate generals, and how to create confusion by opening fire behind the lines; they proved this by shooting one of the camp guards and then shooting up a brothel with the intention of robbing the pimps. At the end of the training these commandos were paid very large sums of cash and released into Greek territory in order to begin the process of destabilising it. Without exception they disappeared with the money and were never heard of again. Francesco and I received more medals for our 'outstanding contribution', and were posted back to our unit.

A few more things happened. One of our own aircraft dropped 'Greek' pamphlets on us, encouraging the Albanians to revolt against us and join the British. We identified the aircraft as one of ours almost immediately, and some of our more stupid soldiers could not understand why we were encouraging our own people to defect. More of our frontier posts were attacked by our own people dressed as Greeks, and some Albanians had potshots taken at them to make them think that they needed us to protect them. Some Albanians actually shot at us as well, and we announced that they had been Greeks. The Governor-General arranged to have his own offices blown up so that the Duce could finally and definitively declare war. He duly did so, shortly after he had ordered a demobilisation that left us with too few troops and no reasonable expectation of reinforcements.

I have related these things as though they are amusing, but really they were acts of lunacy. We had been told that the Greeks were demoralised and corrupt, that they would desert to fight on our side, that the war would be a Blitzkrieg that would be over in seconds, that northern Greece was full of disaffected irredentists who wanted union with Albania; but we only wanted to go home. I only wanted to be in love with Francesco. We were sent off to die, with no transport, no equipment, no tanks worthy of the name, an air force that was mainly in Belgium, insufficient troops, and no officers above the rank of colonel who knew anything about tactics. Our commander refused reinforcements because he would get more credit for a victory with a small army. Another idiot. I did not desert. Perhaps we were all idiots.

It fills me with incalculable bitterness and weariness to describe that campaign. Here in this sunny, secluded island of Cephallonia, with its genial inhabitants and its pots of basil, it seems inconceivable that much of it ever happened. Here in Cephallonia I lounge in the sun and watch dancing competitions between the inhabitants of Lixouri and those of Argostoli. Here in Cephallonia I fill my mind with reveries of Captain Antonio Corelli, a man who, full of mirth, his mind whirling with mandolins, could not be more different from the vanished and beloved Francesco, but whom I love as much.

Passage B

Milo Minderbender, who has graduated from mess officer to international entrepreneur taking money from both sides, has made a mistake in buying the entire Egyptian cotton crop.

Extract 1

M & M Enterprises verged on collapse. Milo cursed himself hourly for his monumental greed and stupidity in purchasing the entire Egyptian cotton crop, but a contract was a contract and had to be honored, and one night, after a sumptuous evening meal, all Milo's fighters and bombers took off, joined in formation directly overhead and began dropping bombs on the group. He had landed another contract with the Germans, this time to bomb his own outfit. Milo's planes separated in a well co-ordinated attack and bombed the fuel stocks and the ordnance dump, the repair hangars and the B-25 bombers resting on the lollipop-shaped hardstands at the field. His crews spared the landing strip and the mess halls so that they could land safely when their work was done and enjoy a hot snack before retiring. They bombed with their landing lights on, since no one was shooting back. They bombed all four squadrons, the officers' club and the Group Headquarters building. Men bolted from their tents in sheer terror and did not know in which direction to turn. Wounded soon lay screaming everywhere. A cluster of fragmentation bombs exploded in the yard of the officers' club and punched jagged holes in the side of the wooden building and in the bellies and backs of a row of lieutenants and captains standing at the bar. They doubled over in agony and dropped. The rest of the officers fled towards the two exits in panic and jammed up the doorways like a dense, howling dam of human flesh as they shrank from going farther.

Extract 2

The loud-speaker overhead began squawking. 'Milo. This is Alvin Brown. I've finished dropping my bombs. What should I do now?'

'Strafe,' said Milo.

'*Strafe?*' Alvin Brown was shocked.

'We have no choice,' Milo informed him resignedly. 'It's in the contract.'

'Oh, okay, then,' Alvin Brown acquiesced. 'In that case I'll strafe.'

This time Milo had gone too far. Bombing his own men and planes was more than even the most phlegmatic observer could stomach, and it looked like the end for him. High-ranking government officials poured in to investigate. Newspapers inveighed against Milo with glaring headlines, and Congressmen denounced the atrocity in stentorian wrath and clamored for punishment. Mothers with children in the service organized into militant groups and demanded revenge. Not one voice was raised in his defense. Decent people everywhere were affronted, and Milo was all washed up until he opened his books to the public and disclosed the tremendous profit he had made. He could reimburse the government for all the people and property he had destroyed and still have enough money left over to continue buying Egyptian cotton. Everybody, of course, owned a share. And the sweetest part of the whole deal was that there really was no need to reimburse the government at all.

'In a democracy, the government is the people,' Milo explained. 'We're people, aren't we? So we might just as well keep the money and eliminate the middleman. Frankly, I'd like to see the government get out of war altogether and leave the whole field to private industry. If we pay the government everything we owe it, we'll only be encouraging government control and discouraging other individuals from bombing their own men and planes. We'll be taking away their incentive.'

Plan

The plan and notes below outline a possible response to this question. There are several ways of approaching the question, of course. Here we keep comparison (AO2ii) at the forefront of the writing all the time, as well as finding opportunities to show the skills appropriate to Assessment Objectives 3 and 4.

Similarities

- 'I have related these things as though they are amusing, but really they were acts of lunacy' – applies to subject matter, style of both novels and passages.

- Aircraft/troops attacking own sides.

- Money as motive for military action, not patriotism – *C22* bombing for pecuniary gain.

- These acts minor in *CCM*, where patriotism sometimes approved, major in *C22*. In *CCM* as result of deceit 'Without exception they disappeared . . .', in *C22* breathtakingly open – Milo justifies the action.

- Both passages show the violence of war as product of attacking own side, and casual attitude to human life – illustrate with quotations from both texts.

Differences

- Even though Yossarian at centre of *C22*, it's more dominated by political concerns than *CCM*, as shown here in the discussion of outcome of bombing. Political black humour. Injury/death presented impersonally 'punched jagged holes . . . in buildings . . . and in the bellies and backs . . .'. Never presented this way in *CCM*.

- *CCM* full of personal voices, as 'I' here, which often deal with love 'I only wanted to be in love with Francesco' – not true of *C22*. *CCM* reminds of beauty, warmth, mirth, love in middle of war, as here – not in *C22*.

- Structure similar, but different. Neither is chronological sequence, but *CCM* more so, though this diary entry (device only in *CCM*) refers to a figure (Captain Corelli) not yet 'met' in novel. 'Forward and back' much more pronounced *C22*. This entry 'placed' only at end of novel, when read in last chapter by Captain Corelli. In *C22* 'It looked like the end for him' is reminder of circularity of novel, which keeps coming back to the death of Snowden.

- Differences in presentation/style.

- Repetition of 'Here in' in last para. of *CCM* emphasises Carlo's stillness, satisfaction, love in this place. Typical tone for Cephallonia.

- In *C22*, sudden shift into violence typical. Irony of contract being 'honored' by attacking own side, and Milo finally advocating his crime as patriotic, because everybody gains. Black humour – this and Alvin accepting strafing – 'It's in the contract' 'Oh, okay, then.' Aircraft hardstands 'lollipop-shaped' – odd suggestion of childishness of murderous attack – part of a sick game.

Intertextuality

- Apart from opening quote, other elements in passages which not only relate to the rest of the text, but to the other text also.

- In *CCM*, incompetence of authorities governing war is also shown in Metaxas and Gandin – and nearly all of the authority figures in *C22*. 'Our commander refused reinforcements . . .' reminds of Colonel Cathcart. Part of anti-war stance of both novels, as is 'We only wanted to go home', 'We were sent home to die' – but figure most embodies this is Yossarian. 'Another idiot. I did not desert. Perhaps we were all idiots' – echoes *C22* characters.

- In *C22*, 'dense howling dam of flesh' might remind of execution/burning scenes in *CCM*.

Importance of passage

- *CCM*: links to rest of novel apart from those mentioned: story of Carlo/Francesco. Carlo's death needed because of structure, and therefore the manner of it – the saving of Corelli. Francesco/Carlo burning watch tower. First appearance of Corelli – this mention gives a context for him before he appears as a character – associated here with love/mirth/music/antidote to war.

- *C22*: Milo's achievements – 'a sumptuous evening meal'. Circularity of novel. 'Everybody . . . owned a share' = Milo's reasoning/excuse for immoral actions in various other episodes.

Evaluation

CCM passage more central? Introduction of central/title character. Link to end of novel. *C22* one of many similar? Perhaps reflects more complex, wider emotional range of Corelli? Though perhaps sentimental too? Does this weaken the impact of an anti-war novel? Is that what it is, though? (*N.B. These points are expressed here, as questions, because you would need to say what you think in your actual answers.*)

---

2 'These novels are very similar: they make you laugh and they make you cry.'

Compare these novels in the light of this remark.

Plan

The plan and notes below outline a possible response to this question. As with question 1, there are several ways of approaching the task, keeping comparison (AO2ii) at the forefront of the writing all the time, as well as finding opportunities to show the skills appropriate to Assessment Objectives 3 and 4.

'Laugh' effect – how produced?

- Farcical action used by both. *C22* – the parade, the attacks on Yossarian by Nately's whore. *CCM* – choral elimination, the pea in Stamatis's ear. At same time, laughter in these episodes in *CCM* is affectionate, unlike *C22*.

- Both laugh at lunacy of generals, etc., as part of anti-war mood, but stronger, more unremitting element in *C22*. In *CCM* even Gandin's death dignified.

- *C22* humour black – Milo's activities, Yossarian's anti-patriotism (qualified in *CCM*), the prevalence of lunatic characters, unlike *CCM*. Examples. Characters extreme – Major Major, Milo, Arfy.

- Good approach to comparing ways the novels make reader laugh at lunacy of war is to compare Yossarian with Captain Corelli – we laugh at quite different things, with different effects. Give examples.

'Cry' effect – how produced?

- Both use violent, graphic language and imagery at times, e.g. executions, burnings in *CCM*, death of Snowden in *C22*. This more effective? – graphic description of guts, structural effect of repetition – Yossarian and reader haunted by it, deepens effect.

- Effect of walk through Rome in 'The Eternal City' in *C22* – bleak, universal (give examples), heightened by late position in structure. Also sudden bursts of violence in *C22*, e.g. horrific death of Kid Sampson.

- But in *CCM* much closer, personal examination of human emotions generally, such as the first killing by Mandras – more likely to produce 'cry' because closer to reader? *CCM* has disappointment in love (not present *C22*) and more personal anguish over loss – Pelagia's loss, death of Carlo, death of Francesco – the effect of this heightened by the juxtaposition of lies Carlo tells to F's mother with the truth. Cry possible also at nobility of death – Carlo. Not possible in *C22*.

Overview/Evaluation

Intentions, attitudes of novels slightly different? Don't criticise writers for what they don't try to do? *CCM* uses longer time perspective for some effects, *C22* doesn't attempt this – but *CCM* also weakened in anti-war effect by too much sentiment? Hard edge of humour and politics of *C22* less likely to produce 'cry', but more laughter – satirical largely – this a smaller element in *CCM*.

Sample questions

Two more sample questions are given below, with some reminders of the sort of approach you should take in answering them.

---

3 Remind yourself of the episode in *Captain Corelli's Mandolin* which occurs in Chapter 24, 'A Most Ungracious Surrender', and begins 'I will illustrate the pride of the populace' and concludes: 'On behalf of His Majesty, King Victor Emmanuel.' (*Passage A*)

Also look at the episode in Chapter 8 of *Catch-22*, 'Lieutenant Scheisskopf,' which begins: 'Now Lieutenant Scheisskopf had confidence enough in his powers to spring his big surprise' and ends 'there were few who did not hail him as a true military genius for his important discovery.' (*Passage B*)

Passage A

Carlo is describing his arrival in Cephallonia, and his first meeting with Captain Corelli.

I will illustrate the pride of the populace by retailing what happened when we asked them to surrender. I had this story from Captain Corelli. He was prone to dramatic exaggeration in the telling of a story because everything about him was original, he was always larger than his circumstance, and he would say things for the sake of their value as amusement, with an ironic disregard for the truth. Generally he observed life with raised eyebrows, and he had none of that fragile self-pride that prevents a man from telling a joke against himself. There were some people who thought him a little mad, but I see him as a man who loved life so much that he did not care what kind of impression he made. He adored children, and I saw him kiss a little girl on the head and whirl her in his arms whilst his whole battery was standing at attention, awaiting his inspection, and he loved to make pretty women giggle by snapping his heels together and saluting them with a military precision so consummate that it came over as a mockery of everything soldierly. When saluting General Gandin the action was sloppy to the point of insolence, so you can see what kind of man he was.

I first came across him in the latrines of the encampment. His battery had a latrine known as 'La Scala' because he had a little opera club that shat together there at the same time every morning, sitting in a row on the wooden plank with their trousers about their ankles. He had two baritones, three tenors, a bass, and a counter-tenor who was much mocked on account of having to sing all the women's parts, and the idea was that each man should expel either a turd or a fart during the crescendos, when they could not be heard above the singing. In this way the indignity of communal defecation was minimised, and the whole encampment would begin the day humming a rousing tune that they had heard wafting out of the heads. My first experience of La Scala was hearing the Anvil Chorus at 7.30 a.m., accompanied by a very prodigious and resolute timpani. Naturally I could not resist going to investigate, and I approached a canvas enclosure that had 'La Scala' painted on it in splashes of blanco. I noticed an appalling and very rank stench, but I went in, only to see a row of soldiers shitting at their perches, red in the face, singing at full heart, hammering at their steel helmets with spoons. I was both confused and amazed, especially when I saw that there was an officer sitting there amongst the men, insouciantly conducting the concert with the aid of a feather in his right hand. Generally one salutes an officer in uniform, especially when he is wearing his cap. My salute was a hurried and incomplete gesture that accompanied my departure – I did not know the regulation that governs the saluting of an officer in uniform who has his breeches at half-mast during a drill that consists of choral elimination in occupied territory.

Subsequently I was to join the opera society, 'volunteered' by the captain after he had heard me singing as I polished my boots, and had realised that I was another baritone. He handed me a piece of paper filched from General Gandin's own order-pad, and on it was written:

TOP SECRET

By Order of HQ, Supergreccia, Bombadier Carlo Piero Guercio is to report for operatic duty at every and any whim of Captain Antonio Corelli of the 33rd Regiment of Artillery, Acqui Division.

Rules of engagement:

1) All those called to regular musical fatigues shall be obliged to play a musical instrument (spoons, tin helmet, comb-and-paper, etc.).

2) Anyone failing persistently to reach high notes shall be emasculated, his testicles to be donated to charitable causes.

3) Anyone maintaining that Donizetti is better than Verdi shall be dressed as a woman, mocked openly before the battery and its guns, shall wear a cooking pot upon his head, and, in extreme cases, shall be required to sing 'Funiculi Funicula' and any other songs about railways that Captain Antonio Corelli shall from time to time see fit to determine.

4) All aficionados of Wagner shall be shot peremptorily, without trial, and without leave of appeal.

5) Drunkenness shall be mandatory only at those times when Captain Antonio Corelli is not buying the drinks.

Signed; General Vecchiarelli, Supreme Commander, Supergreccia, on behalf of His Majesty, King Victor Emmanuel.

Passage B

Now Lieutenant Scheisskopf had confidence enough in his powers to spring his big surprise. Lieutenant Scheisskopf had discovered in his extensive research that the hands of marchers, instead of swinging freely, as was then the popular fashion, ought never to be moved more than three inches from the center of the thigh, which meant, in effect, that they were scarcely to be swung at all.

Lieutenant Scheisskopf's preparations were elaborate and clandestine. All the cadets in his squadron were sworn to secrecy and rehearsed in the dead of night on the auxiliary paradeground. They marched in darkness that was pitch and bumped into each other blindly, but they did not panic, and they were learning to march without swinging their hands. Lieutenant Scheisskopf's first thought had been to have a friend of his in the sheet metal shop sink pegs of nickel alloy into each man's thighbones and link them to the wrists by strands of copper wire with exactly three inches of play, but there wasn't time – there was never enough time – and good copper wire was hard to come by in wartime. He remembered also that the men, so hampered, would be unable to fall properly during the impressive fainting ceremony preceding the marching and that an inability to faint properly might affect the unit's rating as a whole.

And all week long he chortled with repressed delight at the officers' club. Speculation grew rampant among his closest friends.

'I wonder what that Shithead is up to,' Lieutenant Engle said.

Lieutenant Scheisskopf responded with a knowing smile to the queries of his colleagues. 'You'll find out Sunday,' he promised. 'You'll find out.'

Lieutenant Scheisskopf unveiled his epochal surprise that Sunday with all the aplomb of an experienced impresario. He said nothing while the other squadrons ambled past the reviewing stand crookedly in their customary manner. He gave no sign even when the first ranks of his own squadron hove into sight with their swingless marching and the first stricken gasps of alarm were hissing from his startled fellow officers. He held back even then until the bloated colonel with the big fat mustache whirled upon him savagely with a purpling face, and then he offered the explanation that made him immortal.

'Look, Colonel,' he announced. 'No hands.'

And to an audience stilled with awe, he distributed certified photostatic copies of the obscure regulation on which he had built his unforgettable triumph. This was Lieutenant Scheisskopf's finest hour. He won the parade, of course, hands down, obtaining permanent possession of the red pennant and ending the Sunday parades altogether, since good red pennants were as hard to come by in wartime as good copper wire. Lieutenant Scheisskopf was made First Lieutenant Scheisskopf on the spot and began his rapid rise through the ranks. There were few who did not hail him as a true military genius for his important discovery.

Think about the following comparative elements before you write your answer.

1 'a mockery of everything soldierly' applies to both passages. How is military discipline made a mockery of in each passage? Compare them. Think about similar elements in both novels as a whole.

2 People behave absurdly in both passages. Who does so, and what are their motivations? Again, decide how far this is true in the novels as a whole. Which contains more absurdity?

3 What is the attitude of military authority to ordinary soldiers in each passage? Compare the two, focusing on the presentation of authority and the ordinary soldiers in each novel.

4 What is the attitude of the soldiers to military discipline and regulations in each passage?

5 Each passage focuses on a central character as well as 'everything soldierly'. Compare the two main characters, and the ways they are presented. Which of these characters values life and human dignity, and which doesn't?

6 There are various kinds of humour in these passages. Find some examples of these: broad humour/farce/ridicule/irony. Compare the balance of types of humour, and think about the novels as a whole.

4 'These two novels trivialise the horrors of war.'

Compare the novels, giving your view of the extent to which each trivialises war.

This question clearly invites argument, and there are a number of ways you could tackle it, even after you've decided whether you want broadly to agree with the accusation or not. The question clearly addresses AO2ii, and AO4 is also very clear here – you're invited to make a judgement in the light of a critical position. Remember, though, that AO3 is also part of the assessment in this module, so you'll have to find ways to show your understanding of 'the ways writers' choices of form, structure and language shape meanings' as you write.

Here is a sample plan for your answer:

1 A statement of what the issues might be, and of your position in relation to them.

2 A view of the possible reasons for this opinion, comparing the elements of each novel, the way humour is presented and is used.

3 The ways in which each of the novels is not 'trivial', comparing writers' attitudes and methods as well as the 'serious' moments and episodes.

4 Overview/evaluation. A view, developed from the writing you've done, of the balance of seriousness and humour in each novel. A final judgement on each/both of the novels in the light of the opinion given in the question.

Whether you choose to do a passage-based question or not, the mark schemes are the same. You need to know what you have to do in order to do well, and what you have to avoid. Here are some key descriptors which might help:

Assessment Objective 2ii is the dominant objective here. The descriptors for 14–15 marks out of 20, the top of Band 3, are:

- clearly able to evaluate and analyse issues in extracts and whole texts; exploratory; analyses links between and differences of form, structure and language; systematic textual detail.

The descriptors for 0–6 marks, Band 1, are:

- simple narration of extracts; often irrelevant/assertive; factual inaccuracies; reliant on reworked notes; little or no grasp of how language shapes writers' meanings; unplanned, chaotic.

Assessment Objectives 1, 3 and 4 are less important here, but taken together still carry a lot of weight.

The descriptors for 14–15 marks (top of Band 3) are:

- coherent and well-developed lines of argument; pertinent, well-chosen vocabulary showing a command of the technical rules of English; coherent, informed personal response to extracts and whole texts.

The descriptors for 0–6 marks, Band 1, are:

- frequent technical lapses; no obvious line of argument or meaningful discussion of interpretative approaches; narrow range of meanings; confused responses to texts; limited vocabulary; poor deployment of knowledge.

Module 6 Reading for Meaning

This module carries 40% of the final A2 mark, 20% of the final A level mark. The marks are divided amongst the Assessment Objectives like this:

ASSESSMENT OBJECTIVES

AO1 communicate clearly the knowledge, understanding and insight appropriate to literary study, using appropriate terminology and accurate and coherent written expression
(9% of the final A2 mark; 4.5% of the final A Level mark)

AO2ii respond with knowledge and understanding to literary texts of different types and periods, exploring and commenting on relationships and comparisons between literary texts
(7% of the final A2 mark; 3.5% of the final A Level mark)

AO3 show detailed understanding of the ways in which writers' choices of form, structure and language shape meanings
(8% of the final A2 mark; 4% of the final A Level mark)

AO4 articulate independent opinions and judgements, informed by different interpretations of literary texts by other readers
(7% of the final A2 mark; 3.5% of the final A Level mark)

AO5ii evaluate the significance of cultural, historical and other contextual influences on literary texts and study
(9% of the final A2 mark; 4.5% of the final A Level mark)

The purpose of this module

The aim of this module is to test the skills, knowledge and understanding of English Literature you have gained throughout the course, by looking at some unprepared material. In other words, to see how well you can apply the five Assessment Objectives to unfamiliar material. For that reason, all the Assessment Objectives are tested here.

The key preparation for this module is to complete the rest of the course – if you've followed it sensibly, you'll already have a good working knowledge of the requirements of this module, because they're the requirements of the whole course. Here you will be required to look at prose, poetry, drama and non-fiction, and pre-twentieth century as well as twentieth-century literature. This module will test your ability to:

* trace connections between texts

* show knowledge and understanding of form, structure and language

* present your own and others' interpretations of text

* evaluate the significance of contextual influences.

These should come as no surprise to you: you've tackled them all during the course, and they are set out in the Assessment Objective list above.

There are two specific elements to think about in approaching this module. Although the material in the examination is unseen, it is taken from an identified area of English Literature, and you will be expected to have undertaken a course of wide reading in this area, which you will then be able to draw on in the examination. In the first three years of the specification this will be 'War in Literature', with specific emphasis on literature written about and during the First World War. You need to plan your reading and, more importantly, how to read for maximum effect. Secondly, you will need to look closely at the requirements of the exam itself, which are quite different from those of the other modules, in the sense that there are *no set texts*.

Preparing for the module: wide reading

There are many texts you could read which deal with the First World War, some of which you may have studied for GCSE. There are also many texts which deal with other wars, and with war generally. A list of suitable texts is supplied in the specification, and more texts are suggested in the material provided in this section. Before you start reading, though, you need to think very carefully about the purpose of your reading. You're not going to be tested on any of these 'background' texts, after all, – what you are doing is providing yourself with a bank of material which you might refer to in the exam, when you are writing about the extracts provided. It will be useful to measure the extracts against your own reading, in a number of ways. Below (page 143) is a list of features it would be useful to bear in mind as you choose material to read, and then as you read, so that you can provide yourself with a variety of useful information and ideas.

Range of genres

The questions in the exam cover the full range of genres, so you should aim to do the same in your background reading. Here are some of the obvious choices for reading material:

Prose (fiction):

- *Birdsong* (Sebastian Faulks). There are some excerpts from this text in this book, in Module 5.
- *The Regeneration Trilogy* (Pat Barker).
- *Strange Meeting* (Susan Hill).
- *The Ice Cream War* (William Boyd).

Prose (non-fiction):

- *Somme* (Lyn MacDonald). A synopsis of first-hand accounts of the Battle of the Somme.

- *Letters from a Lost Generation* (eds A. Bishop and M. Bostridge). Correspondence between Vera Brittain and three young soldiers, which formed the basis of: *Testament of Youth, Chronicles of Youth, Diaries* (Vera Brittain).

- *Goodbye To All That* (Robert Graves). Autobiography, including his experience as a young officer in the war.

Poetry

- Wilfred Owen, who died in the last days of the war, was arguably the finest war poet, and his work certainly cannot be ignored. Some of his poems are in this book, in Module 5.

- Poems by Siegfried Sassoon should also be read, along with Rupert Brooke, whose patriotic poems are very much at odds with the work of Owen and Sassoon.

- There are many other poets to read whose work is widely anthologised, for example Isaac Rosenberg and Ivor Gurney. There are a number of good anthologies of First World War poetry.

- The publication of the anthology of women's First World War poetry, *Scars Upon My Heart* (ed. Catherine W. Reilly) in 1981 was a breakthrough in the study of literature of the period. Hardly any of the earlier anthologies covering this period had featured women's writing.

- *The Penguin Book of First World War Poetry* (ed. J. Silkin).

Drama

- *Journey's End* (R. C. Sherriff).
- *Not About Heroes* (Stephen MacDonald).
- *Oh What A Lovely War!* (Theatre Workshop).
- *The Accrington Pals* (Peter Whelan).
- *Observe the Sons of Ulster Marching Towards the Somme* (Frank McGuinness).

Collections and commentaries

- *Virago Book of Women and the Great War* (ed. Joyce Marlowe).
- *The Great War and Modern Memory* (ed. Paul Fussell).
- *Women's Writing on the First World War* (ed. Agnes Cardinal).
- *The Great War in British Literature* (Adrian Barlow).

Features of war

When you start reading texts about the war, the first points of comparison you are likely to notice are the features of the war that the writers deal with. A phrase you might come across in the exam is 'Examine how typical in both style and treatment of subject matter these writings are . . .'. The question is asking you to compare the way texts are written, and how they deal with their subjects, with other texts about the First World War – which is why you need a good background of purposeful reading. Identifying features of the war doesn't enable you to write about style and treatment by itself, but nevertheless it is an important first step in making connections in subject matter.

Here are some of the features you might expect to come across, and bear in mind for comparison with other texts:

- trench conditions, including mud, cold, etc.
- fighting and killing – including gas, mines, bayonets, barbed wire as well as shooting
- death in various ways – exposure and drowning as well as combat deaths
- other outcomes – injury and sickness, madness, desertion
- life behind the lines
- life at home – on leave, attitudes of people at home, relationships between home and front via letters, etc.
- political concerns – the conduct and outcome of battles and the war, political objectives, etc.
- love – love expressed in letters to and from home, and the love in comradeship in war.

Feelings and attitudes

Recognising and comparing the feelings and attitudes expressed towards these features in the texts you read takes you one step closer to dealing with 'treatment' of subject matter. An important distinction to make here is between the feelings and attitudes expressed by characters in the text, whether 'real' or otherwise, and the feelings and attitudes of the writers. It is the latter which is more likely to feed into discussion of 'treatment of subject matter', and to lead on to style. This can be seen in Siegfried Sassoon's poem 'Lamentations':

LAMENTATIONS

I found him in the guard-room at the Base.
From the blind darkness I had heard his crying
And blundered in. With puzzled, patient face
A sergeant watched him; it was no good trying
To stop it; for he howled and beat his chest.
And, all because his brother had gone west,

Raved at the bleeding war; his rampant grief
Moaned, shouted, sobbed, and choked, while he was kneeling
Half-naked on the floor. In my belief
Such men have lost all patriotic feeling.

An attitude is expressed in the last line – but whose view is it, and what is it directed towards? It is difficult to believe that the attitude is really that of the poet. A reading of other poems by Sassoon will reveal that this could hardly be the case, and the whole poem implies that the reader cannot take it literally. The soldier is rendered pathetic by the 'blind' darkness in which he is crying, and the poet says that he 'blundered' in, suggesting an awkwardness at intruding on the man's grief. The sergeant is 'puzzled', presumably at the extent of the emotion, and 'patient', presumably he recognises the man's sincerity. The diction of the next few lines emphasises the extremity of the soldier's despair: 'howled', 'raved', 'rampant', 'moaned, shouted, sobbed, and choked'. The 'bleeding war' is ambiguous, both a curse and a literal fact, and the soldier's state and position of 'kneeling/ Half-naked on the floor' emphasises his vulnerability and loss of dignity. In the middle of this, 'all because his brother had gone west' may well be viewed by the reader as sarcasm – 'all because', allied to the casual diction of 'had gone west' obviously belies the depth of the man's feelings. In the face of this, 'In my belief/ Such men have lost all patriotic feeling' becomes deeply sarcastic; the poet is attacking the attitude that could express such a sentiment. This in itself leads to a wider questioning, about the nature and effects of 'patriotic feeling' in the war.

Below is a poem by Wilfred Owen in which similar features can be identified and explored. First read the poem, looking for the feelings and attitudes expressed, and then work through the questions in Activity 1.

THE DEAD-BEAT

He dropped, – more sullenly than wearily,
Lay stupid like a cod, heavy like meat,
And none of us could kick him to his feet;
Just blinked at my revolver, blearily;
– Didn't appear to know a war was on,   5
Or see the blasted trench at which he stared.
'I'll do 'em in,' he whined. 'If this hand's spared,
I'll murder them, I will.'
                                        A low voice said,
'It's Blighty, p'raps, he sees; his pluck's all gone,
Dreaming of all the valiant, that aren't dead: 10
Bold uncles, smiling ministerially;
Maybe his brave young wife, getting her fun
In some new home, improved materially.
It's not these stiffs have crazed him; nor the Hun.'

We sent him down at last, out of the way.   15
Unwounded; – stout lad, too, before that strafe.
Malingering? Stretcher-bearers winked, 'Not half!'

Next day I heard the Doc's well-whiskied laugh:
'That scum you sent last night soon died. Hooray!'

ACTIVITY 1

1 There are a number of features of the war mentioned here. Make a list of
   them and think about:

   • the man's condition

   • the trench

   • the causes of madness

   • the officer's behaviour (first stanza)

   • life at home

   • the doctor, and what his attitude and 'well-whiskied laugh' tell you.

2 Identify the various attitudes expressed in this poem. Think about the
   attitudes of:

   • the officer (first stanza)

   • various people at home

   • the stretcher-bearers

   • the doctor.

3 The 'I' in the last stanza of the poem is clearly an officer's voice – Wilfred
   Owen was an officer in the trenches himself. If you believe that, like
   Sassoon's poem 'Lamentations', the view expressed in the last line is the
   opposite of the poet's view, what evidence can you find in the rest of the
   poem to back this up?

   Look at line 16: who is it who is thinking 'stout lad'?

   Look also at line 18: what is the effect of 'well-whiskied'?

   Think about the title of the poem as well. Whose voice do you think the
   phrase 'The Dead-Beat' belongs to, and what does it reveal about the
   attitude of the speaker?

4 Whose is the 'low voice' (line 8) do you think? If your answer is 'just another
   soldier', does the expression fit? Is this a problem with the poem? Can you
   think of any other interpretation?

You will obviously come across many attitudes in your reading, both of
characters and writers, and trying to categorise them would be futile. But

registering different attitudes to the various features of the war that you read about is certainly worthwhile.

In the activity on 'The Dead-Beat' you identified features of the war, moving towards 'knowledge and understanding' (AO2) and knowledge of context (AO5), and started to 'explore and comment on relationships between literary texts' (AO2). Exploring interpretations of the poem (Question 4) and comparing with another poem (Question 3) leads you towards AO4. The last two suggestions in Question 3 also address 'an understanding of the ways writers' choices of form, structure and language shape meanings' (AO3).

The elements of AO3 need thinking about separately and in detail, though, as they are the key elements of 'style' which you will be tested on in the exam. Of course, there are too many possible variations here to think about them all, but there are some elements which appear regularly in First World War literature, and which may therefore feature either in the examination extracts, or can be used in comparison or contrast to them.

Form

Form goes beyond simply the broad forms of the three genres of prose, drama and poetry. Non-fiction *prose* forms you may come across regularly are letters, diaries, journals, and other forms of first-hand accounts, as in *Somme* and *Letters from a Lost Generation*. Because of the nature of the First World War and the writing associated with it, these forms are used by fiction writers too.

The nature of the war also influences the forms taken by *drama*, as rendering the realities of trench warfare on stage in a naturalistic way is clearly a difficult task, the only enduring example being *Journey's End*. The war of 1914–18 became modern, in the sense that it became increasingly mechanised and fought at a distance; this, and the sheer scale of the battlefield, made it much more difficult to represent than smaller-scale conflicts in predominantly hand-to-hand battle. Of course, Shakespeare could not depict the whole of the battle of Agincourt, for instance; but by showing snapshots of situations in various parts of the field the whole picture could be suggested with reasonable accuracy. This could not be done with the subsequent involvement of tanks and aircraft, and long-distance shelling. Later wars than the First World War have hardly been the subject of stage drama at all, except in miniature in such plays as *The Long, the Short and the Tall* by Willis Hall, which concerns a platoon of British soldiers in the Malayan jungle during the Second World War. The resources of film have proved more suitable to showing modern warfare. It would be easy to list dozens of films about the Second World War and the Vietnam War, for instance, but few plays come to mind.

Dramatists have therefore used various techniques to cope with the problems of portraying the First World War on stage: the use of voices, stage positions and sound in *Not About Heroes*, the surreal elements of *The Accrington Pals*, and the range of strategies developed by Joan Littlewood with the Theatre Workshop group for *Oh What A Lovely War!*. Forms here include song, dance, and slides, as well as the device of seeing the war through a particular dramatic setting which is itself a dramatic form.

The following extract from Peter Whelan's *The Accrington Pals* illustrates some of the problems and solutions. *The Accrington Pals* was one of the volunteer regiments raised in the early years of the First World War. The Pals went into action on the first day of the Battle of the Somme, 1 July 1916. Between 7.20 a.m. and 8.30 a.m., 584 of the 720 men were killed, wounded or missing, and there was a total of 60,000 British casualties on that day. The play shows the recruiting in the town, and intercuts action in battle with life 'at home', as the women and children of the town hear initial optimistic reports, before the awful truth is known.

contrasts life at home.

RALPH   I'm not going to drown. Shot or blown to bits but not drowned. Loose your straps. I reckon if you're out of your pack quick enough and get it under your feet you might keep up. But tie your water bottle separate. Fuck all use not drowning if you die of thirst! Oh these straps. I'll never get out fast enough.

TOM   You could cut them.

RALPH   I've tried. Bayonet's too blunt!

TOM   Borrow this.

RALPH   That's your leather knife . . . What will you do?

TOM   Oh aye . . .

RALPH   What you made of Tom? You going over there to talk philosophy with them?

TOM   There's a lot of good German philosophers.

RALPH   Well, there's fuck-all of them over there! Wake up Arthur, get up.

VOICE   [*off*] Move up nine platoon. Move!

ARTHUR   [*to his pet pigeon England's Glory*] Now sweet . . . now my beauty . . . the sun is shining and the air is clear . . .

RALPH   Hold on to me Tom. Oh mother, I've got the movies. Push me if you see me falling back . . . don't let them see me go back. Christ I'm clasped so tight I'll bust!

[*CSM Rivers dashes in to join them.*]

RIVERS   Heads down! Get your heads down! Seven-thirty ack-emma . . . mines detonating.

VOICES   Stand by! Stand by! Take cover!

RIVERS   Brace yourselves!

A vast deep roaring sound as the Hawthornden Ridge mine goes off. They cower and sway as the shock waves go through the trench.

Well the Pals! Next stop, Serre for Beaumont Hamel, Bapaume and Berlin!

[*Shouts off*] Mr Williams, sir! Move your platoon up! [*Quietly, to Tom*] Think of her, shall we, Hackford . . . think of her? If you lose your officers don't make for the gaps in the wire . . . Jerry's got his Spandaus trained on the gaps and he'll rip you to pieces . . . cut your own; understood? Got your wire cutters?

TOM   Yes sir.

RIVERS   Let glory shine from your arseholes today boys. Rise on the whistle . . . dress from the right . . . rifles at the port . . . go steady and we'll be drinking schnappes and eating sausages by sundown. Boggis . . . let's have a prayer.

ARTHUR   Oh God . . . do you smile still? Do you smile to see your handiwork?

Whistles begin to blow around the theatre, merging into one another.

RIVERS   Over we go . . . stay in line . . . right marker!

VOICES   Come on the Pals. Up the Accringtons! Nine platoon! Ten platoon! With me, with me, with me! Dress from the right. Leave that man! Leave him!

They go over the top. Mingling with the machine guns stuttering we hear an awkward, heavy piano introduction to Edward German's 'Oh Peaceful England' being played. Eva appears in her Britannia costume. She is singing at the fund raising concert. She looks tense and nervous . . . almost angry. She begins to sing.

EVA   [*sings*]

Oh peaceful England, while I my watch am keeping,
Thou like Minerva weary of war art sleeping.
Sleep on a little while and in thy slumber smile.
While thou art sleeping I my watch am keeping.
Sword and buckler by thy side, rest on the shore of battle-tide,
Which like the ever hungry sea, howls round this Isle.
Sleep till I awaken thee, and in thy slumber smile.
England, fair England, well hast thou earned thy slumber,
Yet though thy bosom no breast-plate now encumber . . .

Suddenly she breaks off. She's lost the next line. The accompanyist falters. Eva begins to shake with fury at the situation she's put herself in. She exclaims something and runs off.

The playwright can show some of the conditions and feelings of the war through the small group of soldiers, but the size of the field can only be suggested by Rivers shouting offstage to the next platoon in the line. The nature of the battle has to be suggested by sound effects, and when the men go over the top realistic portrayal is impossible. Later in the play a dream-like, surreal sequence of action is used; Whelan ends the scene by cutting to a 'home' scene which suggests loss and a horrible mistake, while remaining in the context of war and patriotism – German's famous patriotic song becomes ironic here. There are a number of other features of the war in the extract which you should recognise by now: the trench conditions, the expectation of death, thoughts of home, attitude to the enemy, and despair of religion.

Poetry of the time used the full range of poetic forms available, and in addition much poetry has been written later, using more modern techniques. There was one significant development in poetic form which you should look at. This was the development by Wilfred Owen of half-rhyme, sometimes called pararhyme or consonantal rhyme, in which the vowel sounds are not the same, but the consonants are. For example, 'moan' and 'blown' rhyme, because the vowel sounds are the same; 'moan' and 'mourn' don't rhyme – the vowel sounds are different – but there is clearly a strong link between the sounds of the two words, as the consonants are the same. Owen found that this rhyme form was more 'in tune' with the destruction and despair that he wanted to write about than the more harmonious effect of full rhyme. With 'moan' and 'mourn', for example, the sound actually deepens. Owen made use of this pair of words several times, along with others which deepened the tone. His technique has affected the writing of poetry profoundly since the time in which he was writing, but during the war most writers were oblivious to it, as Owen's poetry was not published until very late in or after the war.

Here is an example of this technique at work, from 'Strange Meeting':

> With a thousand pains that vision's face was grained;
> Yet no blood reached there from the upper ground,
> And no guns thumped, or down the flues made moan.
> 'Strange friend,' I said, 'here is no cause to mourn.'

The 'moan/mourn' pair is used here, and the effect is increased by the pairing of 'grained/ground', another step down in sound. (The next pair in the poem is 'years/yours'.) Owen uses other resources of form here to deepen the effect. The long 'a' sound of 'grained' is the third in the same line; the assonance of 'pains', 'face', and 'grained' makes the reader feel the pain. The sound of the next line immediately deepens even before 'ground', with 'no', 'blood' and 'upper', the latter being the first of four 'u' sounds in these lines.

Here is another example of a complex pattern of sounds and half-rhymes, in the last verse of Owen's poem 'Insensibility'. Read the lines and work through Activity 2.

But cursed are dullards whom no cannon stuns,
That they should be as stones;
Wretched are they, and mean
With paucity that never was simplicity.
By choice they made themselves immune
To pity and whatever moans in man
Before the last sea and the hapless stars;
Whatever mourns when many leave these shores;
Whatever shares
The eternal reciprocity of tears.

ACTIVITY 2

1 Pick out the first half-rhyme in these lines.

2 Where is the half-rhyme for 'mean'? (Read the lines very carefully.)

3 'Simplicity' doesn't seem to have an obvious rhyme – but check all the lines here. There are in fact two echoes of it – can you find them?

4 Where are the half-rhymes for 'stars' and 'shores'?

5 Whereabouts in the lines does the 'moans/mourns' half-rhyme appear? What else echoes this pairing?

6 The poem is about 'insensibility' – the various ways in which soldiers in the war became insensible to suffering, through fatigue, madness, loss of senses, or just simple-mindedness. This last verse attacks those who choose not to feel. Given this, why does Owen choose 'tears' as the last word of the poem? ('Reciprocity' means 'sharing' or 'common feeling'.)

The choice of this word – 'insensibility' – reflects how Owen has used all three elements of 'form, language and structure to shape meaning'.

Structure

You will probably come across various distinctive uses of *structure* in your reading, without any of them being characteristic of either war literature or specifically First World War literature. This war was such a significant event in the history of the twentieth century, however, its effects were so far-reaching, and its nature so distressing, that writers have continued to write about it ever since. A desire to 'place' the war experience, both historically and in human terms, produces structures like that of the novel *Birdsong*, which focuses on times before, during and after the war years, which are the defining experiences for all the characters, even those born after the war itself had ended.

One of the aims of *war poets* such as Owen and Sassoon was to 'tell the truth' about their experiences, as they felt the truth was not known, or being told, at home. This aim is often achieved through very direct or abrupt endings, in other words, the meaning is shaped by the structure. Here are some examples:

> O Jesus, make it stop!
>
> (S. Sassoon, 'Attack')

> Sneak home and pray you'll never know
> The hell where youth and laughter go.
>
> (S. Sassoon, 'Suicide in the Trenches')

> Oh what made fatuous sunbeams toil
> To break earth's sleep at all?
>
> (W. Owen, 'Futility')

> Snatching after us who smote them, brother,
> Pawing us who dealt them war and madness.
>
> (W. Owen, 'Mental Cases')

> 'E's wounded, killed, and pris'ner, all the lot,
> The bloody lot all rolled in one. Jim's mad.
>
> (W. Owen, 'The Chances')

Structures in many *drama texts* work in the same way, seeking to remind audiences of the desperation of the war through dramatic means at key points. Below are two short extracts from R. C. Sherriff's *Journey's End*. The first is the opening to Act 3, Scene 1, and the second is the end of the play, when Raleigh is lying fatally wounded in the dug-out as the men prepare to go over the top.

Extract 1

The following day, towards sunset. The earth wall of the trench outside glows with a light that slowly fades with the sinking sun.

Stanhope is alone, wandering to and fro across the dug-out. He looks at the steps for a moment, crosses to the table, and glances down at the map. He looks anxiously at his watch, and, going to the servant's dug-out, calls:

STANHOPE   Mason!

Extract 2

RALEIGH   Could we have a light? It's – it's so frightfully dark and cold.

STANHOPE   [*rising*] Sure! I'll bring a candle and get another blanket.

[*Stanhope goes to the left-hand dug-out, and Raleigh is alone, very still and quiet, on Osborne's bed. The faint rosy glow of the dawn is deepening to an angry red. The grey night sky is dissolving, and the stars begin to go. A tiny sound comes from where Raleigh is lying – something between a sob and a moan. Stanhope comes back with a blanket. He takes a candle from the table and carries it to Raleigh's bed. He puts it on the box beside Raleigh and speaks cheerfully.*]

Is that better, Jimmy? [*Raleigh makes no sign.*] Jimmy . . .

[*Still Raleigh is quiet. Stanhope gently takes his hand. There is a long silence. Stanhope lowers Raleigh's hand to the bed, rises, and takes the candle back to the table. He sits on the bench behind the table with his back to the wall, and stares listlessly across at the boy on Osborne's bed. The solitary candle-flame throws up the lines on his pale, drawn face, and the dark shadows under his tired eyes. The thudding of the shells rises and falls like an angry sea.*

A Private Soldier comes scrambling down the steps, his round, red face wet with perspiration, his chest heaving for breath.]

SOLDIER   Message from Mr Trotter, sir – will you come at once.

[*Stanhope gazes round at the soldier – and makes no other sign.*]

Mr Trotter, sir – says will you come at once!

[*Stanhope rises stiffly and takes his helmet from the table.*]

STANHOPE   All right, Broughton, I'm coming.

[*The soldier turns and goes away.*

Stanhope pauses for a moment by Osborne's bed and lightly runs his fingers over Raleigh's tousled hair. He goes stiffly up the steps, his tall figure black against the dawn sky.

The shelling has risen to a great fury. The solitary candle burns with a steady flame, and Raleigh lies in the shadows. The whine of a shell rises to a shriek and bursts on the dug-out roof. The shock stabs out the candle-flame; the timber props of the door cave slowly in, sandbags fall and block the passage to the open air.

There is darkness in the dug-out. Here and there the red dawn glows through the jagged holes of the broken doorway.

Very faintly there comes the dull rattle of machine-guns and the fevered spatter of rifle fire.]

ENDS

ACTIVITY 3

Many of the choices the playwright makes here are structural. Look at the following features, and their effects on the audience.

1 Look at the lighting in the first extract. What does this time of day, and the 'sinking sun' suggest? What is Stanhope preoccupied with, and how does that connect with the context and the battle to come?

2 Look at the lighting at the beginning of the second extract. What does the 'angry red' of the dawn suggest? What does the disappearance of the stars suggest?

3 Look at the effect of the candle in the second extract. It is one light in the darkness. What does its extinction symbolise?

4 Sherriff chooses the end of the play to show Raleigh's death. What reasons could he have for doing this? Think about the structure of the play.

5 Look at all the stage directions for sound, and decide why each sound has to come at that exact moment. Why does Sherriff want the shells to sound 'like an angry sea'?

6 In the last minute of the play, Sherriff introduces a 'private soldier' who has not appeared before. Why does he do this? Why does the writer want Stanhope silhouetted against the dawn sky?

7 What does the final scene in the play, including sound, suggest to the audience? Remember that the performance might well end with lights fading to black.

Prose often spells out meanings rather than suggesting them, as the ending of Sherriff's play does. Even in the usually prosaic form of the *letter*, though, writers wanted to draw the lessons from what they were experiencing and shaped their material accordingly.

Here is the end of a letter written by Vera Brittain to her brother, Edward Brittain, in February 1916:

I would like to think of you as never forgetting that one day the War will end and the things that used to matter will matter again; even if you are not to see them I still think it is better to remember, for otherwise your work & life is lived only for the moment and not for all time. And as the effects of this War will be for all time the people who are playing their part in it will play that part for all time too, and to remember this seems to make one's lot – whether it be life or work or horror or death – so much more worthwhile.

Language

From your work on language during the course, you'll be well aware of the many resources writers use to shape meanings, for example diction, syntax, imagery, sounds. Some of these resources are more widely used in First World War literature than others because of the nature of the conflict and the attitudes towards it. Some of them are discussed below.

Use of dialogue in poetry

Many poets wanted to show convincingly the voices of 'common soldiers'. Owen's poem 'The Chances', quoted on page 152, is one example. Other voices were represented too, such as those of officers and women.

Questions

The nature and the length of the war led people to question many things – the conduct of the war, the motives of generals and politicians, religion, and the purpose of life itself – and this was inevitably reflected in literature.

Here are the opening and closing lines of 'Afterwards' by Margaret Postgate Cole:

> Oh, my beloved, shall you and I
> Ever be young again, be young again?

and

> What use is it to you? What use
> To have your body lying here
> In Sheer, underneath the larches?

The last two lines of Owen's 'Futility' are:

> Oh what made fatuous sunbeams toil
> To break earth's sleep at all?

Questions about the purpose of life also appear in the letters of the time, and the questions were often much more immediate here, as in this letter from Lieutenant Cyril Drummond, written on 30 June 1916:

> Lying beside a pile of boxes was the body of a soldier who had been killed earlier in the day. He was covered by a blanket, but one corner was awry, exposing an arm, torn, shattered, and dusty. Suddenly, for the first time, the thought crossed my mind, 'Shall I be looking like that this time tomorrow?'

Exclamations

For much the same reasons as questions, exclamations are often found in contemporary texts, echoing strength of feeling. The lines from 'Futility' above, though technically a rhetorical question, are really more of an exclamation. 'Oh Jesus, make it stop!' (in Sassoon's 'Attack', quoted on page 151) is certainly an exclamation. The same feeling often appeared in letters, as in this ending to a letter from Vera to Edward Brittain on 8 March 1916:

> But if I escape Zeppelins at home, and torpedoes, enteric or dysentery abroad, I promise you to go to Uppingham on behalf of us all . . . And as I told you before you went out, if the War spares me, it will be my one aim to immortalise in a book the story of us four, with the friendship of the Three Musketeers playing so large a part . . . Just as you, if you come through, will immortalise it all in music. Oh! If only it could *end*! We are all so weary.

Religious diction and imagery

Because of the strength of feeling and despair occasioned by the war, religion was frequently either appealed to or questioned. In 'Sacrament' by Margaret Sackville, for instance, she questions the actions of God in sacrificing lives, through the imagery of the sacrament, in the third verse:

> This wine of awful sacrifice outpoured;
>   This bread of life – of human lives. The Press
> Is overflowing, the Wine-Press of the Lord! . . .
>   Yet doth he tread the foaming grapes no less.

In the sacrament, wine and bread represent the blood and body of Christ. Sackville is explicit in saying that the 'bread of life' here means 'human lives', and that the wine is not just the wine of sacrifice, but 'awful'. The emotive effect is enhanced by the word 'outpoured', suggesting volume, placed at the end of the line. The idea of excess blood is picked up by the metaphor of 'the Wine-Press of the Lord' overflowing, and given further impact by the final image of Christ wantonly continuing to tread the grapes. The grapes are human beings, of course, and 'foaming' in this context gives an awful vision of foaming blood.

Owen's 'At a Calvary near the Ancre' and Sassoon's 'The Redeemer' are both powerful accounts of Christ on the battlefield, although the former also echoes the contempt that many soldiers had for the actions of churchmen in the war, as does another poem by Sassoon, 'They'.

Romantic v. realistic

There is a sharp distinction, particularly in poetry, between those writers who perceived the actions of the war as romantic, and therefore used language to portray it in this way, and those whose writing reflects a desire to paint the details of war as graphically and realistically as possible, to suggest the degradation and futility of war. The terms 'romantic' and 'realistic' are in common usage here, but are different to the literary concept of Romanticism.

One of the most famous patriotic war poems, which depends heavily on its romantic diction and imagery, is 'The Soldier', by Rupert Brooke. In this poem, the English soldier's body is 'a richer dust' in 'some corner of a foreign field'.

Here is the opening to Brooke's 'The Dead':

> Blow out, you bugles, over the rich Dead!
>   There's none of these so lonely and poor of old,
>   But, dying, has made us rarer gifts than gold.

By contrast, here is the description of a gas victim in 'Dulce Et Decorum Est', a direct attack by Owen on patriotism:

> And watch the white eyes writhing in his face,
> His hanging face, like a devil's sick of sin;
> If you could hear, at every jolt, the blood
> Come gargling from the froth-corrupted lungs . . .

Here is an extract from *Goodbye To All That* by Robert Graves:

> Going and coming, by the only possible route, I passed by the bloated and stinking corpse of a German with his back propped against a tree. He had a green face, spectacles, close-shaven hair; black blood was dripping from the nose and beard. I came across two other unforgettable corpses: a man of the South Wales Borderers and one of the Lehr regiment had succeeded in bayoneting each other simultaneously. A survivor of the fighting told me later that he had seen a young soldier of the Fourteenth Royal Welch bayoneting a German in parade-ground style, automatically exclaiming: 'In, out, on guard!'

In Brooke's poem, an emblem of military and patriotic feeling – the bugle – is invoked in an exclamation, over the 'rich Dead!' The upper case 'D' in itself glorifies the dead soldiers, who are 'rich'. This is not just heightened language –

picked up again in 'rarer' and 'gold' – it also suggests that soldiers who were 'lonely' and 'poor' are somehow enriched and enriching others by their deaths. This is further emphasised by the weight of the rhyming couplet falling on 'gold'.

The other two extracts are quite different in attitude. Owen's poem is a direct attack on the attitude of Brooke, and here he spells out exactly the details of death in the effect of the gas on the eyes, the face, the blood and the lungs of the soldier. The words 'writhing', 'hanging', 'gargling' and 'froth-corrupted' are deliberately emotive, heightened by the repetition of 'his face', as though the viewer could not take his eyes from the awful sight, and the repulsive idea of 'like a devil's sick of sin'.

Graves, though not using the poetic resources of Owen, nevertheless signals the same attitude in similar ways. The corpse is 'bloated' and 'stinking', with a 'green face' and 'black blood [. . .] dripping from the nose' – a reminder of Owen's description, and far removed from the 'rich' language and attitude of Brooke. The mutually bayoneted figures are grotesque, and in both these recollections the German corpses are equivalent to the British; there is no sense of 'rarer gifts than gold' being given to the countrymen of one side.

The poem below shows how language can be used to *suggest* things, as well as stating them directly. Ivor Gurney was both a poet and a composer, who served as a private soldier in France with his local regiment, the Gloucesters. Read the poem, and attempt the questions which follow in Activity 4.

THE SILENT ONE

Who died on the wires, and hung there, one of two –
Who for his hours of life had chattered through
Infinite lovely chatter of Bucks accent;
Yet faced unbroken wires; stepped over, and went,
A noble fool, faithful to his stripes – and ended.
But I weak, hungry, and willing only for the chance
Of line – to fight in the line, lay down under unbroken
Wires, and saw the flashes, and kept unshaken.
Till the politest voice – a finicking accent, said:
'Do you think you might crawl through, there; there's a hole.' In the
    afraid
Darkness, shot at; I smiled, as politely replied –
'I'm afraid not, Sir.' There was no hole, no way to be seen.
Nothing but chance of death, after tearing of clothes.
Kept flat, and watched the darkness, hearing bullets whizzing –
And thought of music – and swore deep heart's deep oaths
(Polite to God –) and retreated and came on again,
Again retreated – and a second time faced the screen.

ACTIVITY 4

1 Who is 'The Silent One' of the title, do you think? There are at least two interpretations. Find evidence to support each one, and then see if you can think of any more.

2 How does Gurney present the soldier who has died on the wire? Think about what his attitude on the wire might suggest, and what the five adjectives used about him convey about the surviving soldier's attitude to him.

3 What features of trench warfare are referred to in this poem?

4 What does the dialogue tell you about the soldier and the officer? What does each of the three forms of the word 'polite' suggest?

5 Look for all the repetitions of words, language forms or actions used in the last six lines. Taken together, what do they say to you about the nature of the conflict?

Contexts

Assessment Objective 5ii on contexts requires you to 'evaluate the significance of cultural, historical and other contextual influences on literary texts and study'. The over-arching context here is the First World War, of course, but within that there are a number of other contexts which specifically influence individual writers and their texts. Below are some of the contexts which you should recognise in your reading, and which you can then refer to in the exam.

Social

The central social context in most of the writing during and about this war relates to class, and reflects the stratified class system of the time. It emerges chiefly in the attitudes of ordinary soldiers, officers and generals to each other. In Gurney's poem 'The Silent One', consider what the 'polite' exchange of words masks – what the soldiers are being asked to do, and the attitudes towards class differences that lie behind it.

The differences between ranks also included differences between field officers such as Owen and Sassoon and those behind the lines, as reflected in this poem by Sassoon:

BASE DETAILS

If I were fierce, and bald, and short of breath,
    I'd live with scarlet Majors at the Base,
And speed glum heroes up the line to death.
    You'd see me with my puffy petulant face,
Guzzling and gulping in the best hotel,
    Reading the Roll of Honour. 'Poor young chap,'

I'd say – 'I used to know his father well;
  Yes, we've lost heavily in this last scrap.'
And when the war is done and youth stone dead,
I'd toddle safely home and die – in bed.

Class is a significant context for the writing here, not only because of what it says, but because Sassoon himself belonged to the same class as many of the 'scarlet Majors'. Similarly, the outburst of the writer of the following diary entry (from *Tommy Goes to War* by Malcolm Brown), Sapper Garfield Powell of the Royal Engineers, is strengthened by his own background. Powell had a B.Sc. in Chemistry and Mathematics but as a miner's son was not officer material.

As an army we are darned badly treated. Officers claim to get leave every three months and get it. Battalion and Company Sergeant-Majors claim leave every four months and again get it (being called 'Sir' by their inferiors in rank not being sufficient sop to their self-love). In what army (barring the national armies of Germany or Russia) would such a system be in vogue? The officers in most regiments take very little more risk than their privates. Their bodies are not fatigued by constant and hard work and they are no more useful to the Army than privates. Why should the fools in higher command allow it? Why should 'gentlemen' take it as nothing less than their due? Ay, what fools we all are!

The significance of the context of class, and not just officer/ordinary soldier, becomes much clearer towards the end of this piece.

Historical

Although the war itself lasted only four years, which is a short period in history, much changed during this time, even though the lines of battle hardly moved. Early optimism, which produced more optimistic, romantic literary responses, was replaced by the hard slog of the trenches, and after 1916 by a slaughter which became increasingly mechanistic as the new instruments of destruction appeared on the battlefields. The period being written about, therefore, is a significant contextual influence on the writing. Similarly, these writing after the war began to view the war differently, as the surviving combatants struggled to come to terms with 'ordinary' life. This is shown in this extract from Sassoon's 'A Footnote to the War':

But how can I co-ordinate this room –
Music on piano, pictures, shelves of books,
And Sunday morning peace – with him for whom
Nine years ago the world wore such wild looks?
How can my brain join up with the plutonian
Cartoon? . . . The trench; and a fair-haired Cameronian

Propped in his pool of blood while we were throwing
Bombs at invisible Saxons . . . War's a mystery
Beyond my retrospection.

The significance of the context here could hardly be greater; the writer's problem is that in 'ordinary' life the war is inescapable for him, and continues to shape his thoughts and his writing.

Writer's biography and gender

Given the significance of class, rank and period, the *biography* of any writer of the time is bound to be a significant contextual influence. *Gender* is also a very significant contextual influence. Some of the women's poetry of the time shows women in war-time occupations such as nursing, as in Mary Henderson's 'An Incident' (see page 180), and munitions work, as in Mary Gabrielle Collins's poem 'Women at Munitions Making'. The use of women for this sort of work was highly significant in a political and historical context, as many commentators saw it as an important step on the road to women's suffrage. Suffragettes such as Mrs Pankhurst also played a key role as pacifists, and this is reflected in literature too. Much of the poetry, though, simply reflects the feelings of women 'left behind', as in this poem by Gabrielle Elliott. Read the poem below, and work through Activity 5 that follows.

PIERROT GOES TO WAR

In the sheltered garden, pale beneath the moon,
(Drenched with swaying fragrance, redolent with June!)
There, among the shadows, some one lingers yet –
Pierrot, the lover, parts from Pierrette.

Bugles, bugles, bugles, blaring down the wind,
Sound the flaming challenge – *Leave your dreams behind!*
Come away from shadows, turn your back on June –
Pierrot, go forward to face the golden noon!

In the muddy trenches, black and torn and still,
(How the charge swept over, to break against the hill!)
Huddled in the shadows, boyish figures lie –
They whom Death, saluting, called upon to die.

Bugles, ghostly bugles, whispering down the wind –
Dreams too soon are over, gardens left behind.
Only shadows linger, for love does not forget –
Pierrot goes forward – but what of Pierrette?

ACTIVITY 5

Only the last line is a clear plea from the woman's point of view, although the writer has structured the poem so that this plea remains in the reader's mind. The contrasts in the woman's and the man's situation are implied in other ways, as well. Look for the contrasts between:

- the first verse and the third verse

- the lines in brackets

- the different times of year mentioned or hinted at

- the different implications of 'shadows'

- the two mentions of bugles, and the sounds they make

- the poet's references to nature.

Is war, or love, or gender the most significant context here, do you think?

Literary

There are a number of literary contexts for the work of this period. Just as the war proved a watershed in society and history, it affected the development of literature, as writers strove to find new ways of expressing what they saw and felt. The old ways would not do. The difference between the writing of the pre-war years and post-war writing is huge, and is a study in itself. The shift in the poetry of Thomas Hardy, who spans this time period, and the style and attitude of the early war 'patriotic' poems such as those of Rupert Brooke, as shown on pages 156–7, against the later poets, are interesting literary contexts. The development can be seen most clearly, perhaps, in Owen's poetry. At the beginning of the war his poems were still very clearly imitations of Keats, but by the end of the war he was writing in the preface for his planned collection of poems, 'Above all I am not concerned with poetry'. In other words, he had found his own voice. He had become determined to write poetry that 'the dullest Tommy' could understand. His specific literary legacy, apart from the poems themselves, was the use of half-rhyme, as discussed on pages 149–50.

Pre-twentieth-century war literature

The specification requires that this module should also include pre-twentieth-century literature. As the area of literature for the first three years of the specification is First World War literature, it follows that you will be asked to compare a pre-twentieth-century extract with one or more of the First World War extracts, to think about the different ways the writers present war, and to offer a view about them. This offers you a very wide choice – for example, you could look at Shakespeare's treatment of war in many of his plays, or at texts about the American Civil War or the Boer War.

The poem below, 'The Due of the Dead' by W. M. Thackeray, was set in the Crimean War, as was 'The Charge of the Light Brigade' by Tennyson. You could look at similarities and differences between the two poems. The most important thing to bear in mind, however, is that when you are reading pre-twentieth-century literature you should choose and explore texts which can be compared to a work of literature from the later period.

Read the poem below, by W. M. Thackeray (1811–63), and work through Activity 6.

THE DUE OF THE DEAD

I sit beside my peaceful hearth,
  With curtains drawn and lamp trimmed bright
I watch my children's noisy mirth;
  I drink in home, and its delight.

I sip my tea, and criticise
  The war, from flying rumours caught;
Trace on the map, to curious eyes,
  How here they marched, and there they fought.

In intervals of household chat,
  I lay down strategic laws;
Why this manoeuvre, and why that;
  Shape the event, or show the cause.

Or, in smooth dinner-table phrase,
  'Twixt soup and fish, discuss the fight;
Give to each chief his blame or praise;
  Say who was wrong and who was right.

Meanwhile o'er Alma's bloody plain
  The scathe of battle has rolled by –
The wounded writhe and groan – the slain
  Lie naked staring to the sky.

The out-worn surgeon plies his knife,
  Nor pauses with the closing day;
While those who have escaped with life
  Find food and fuel as they may.

And when their eyes in sleep they close,
  After scant rations duly shared,
Plague picks his victims out, from those
  Whom chance of battle may have spared.

Still when the bugle sounds the march,
  He tracks his prey through steppe and dell;
Hangs fruit to tempt the throats that parch,
  And poisons every stream and well.

All this with gallant hearts is done;
  All this with patient hearts is borne:
And they by whom the laurel's won
  Are seldom they by whom 'tis worn.

No deed, no suffering of the war,
    But wins us fame, or spares us ill:
Those noble swords, though drawn afar,
    Are guarding English homesteads still.

Owe we a debt to these brave men,
    Unpaid by aught that's said or sung;
By leaders from a ready pen,
    Or phrases from a flippant tongue.

The living, England's hand may crown
    With recognition, frank and free;
With titles, medals and renown;
    The wounded shall our pensioners be.

But they, who meet a soldier's doom –
    Think you, it is enough, good friend,
To plant the laurel at their tomb,
    And carve their names – and there an end?

No. They are gone: but there are left
    Those they loved best while they were here –
Parents made childless, babes bereft,
    Desolate widows, sisters dear.

All these let grateful England take;
    And, with a large and liberal heart,
Cherish, for her plain soldiers' sake,
    And of her fullness give them part.

Fold them within her sheltering breast;
    Their parent, husband, brother prove.
That so the dead may be at rest,
    Knowing those cared for whom they love.

ACTIVITY 6

1 The setting of the first five verses is at home in England, discussing the progress of war. How does Thackeray emphasise how far the narrator is removed from the war itself? Can you think of any First World War texts which deal with this setting in a similar way?

2 The next four verses deal with the horrors of war. Compare Thackeray's treatment of the subject with that in any First World War text(s) that you have read.

3 Plague is personified over six lines in these verses. Can you think of any similar use of personification in the First World War literature you have read? If you can't, read 'The Next War', by Wilfred Owen. Which of the personifications seems more effective, and why?

4   The next six verses deal with military honours and decorations. What attitudes does Thackeray express here? What attitudes, either similar or different, have you come across in your reading of First World War literature?

5   The feelings and attitudes of those left behind also feature strongly in these verses. Compare any of these with similar thoughts expressed in the First World War texts you have read, being careful to think about *how* the thoughts are expressed as well as the actual ideas.

6   How do you respond to the patriotism of the last two verses? Compare the attitude and expression here to Rupert Brooke's 'The Soldier'.

   • Do you consider this poem to be romantic in nature?

   • Is it far removed from First World War poetry in attitudes and style?

   • Is the form successful, in your view?

   • Think of any other comparisons you might make with the First World War texts you have looked at.

Further sample extracts and activities

Over the next few pages you will find more poems and extracts from First World War literature. They provide additional reading in prose, drama and poetry, but also give you the opportunity to compare and contrast them with other texts you have read. Texts 5, 6 and 7 are by women who were writing at the time of the First World War.

With each extract, try to answer the following questions once you have read and re-read each piece. You could also use these questions as a useful checklist for any other relevant reading you have done.

1   What features of the war can you identify in the text?

2   Identify the feelings and attitudes in the text, being careful to differentiate between the writer's attitude and the attitude of characters, whether real or imagined, in the text.

3   How has the writer used form, structure and language to shape his or her meanings?

4   What contexts can you see, and how significant are they to your reading and understanding of the text?

5   Having worked through the questions above, compare and contrast your findings about the text with other First World War texts, or pre-twentieth-century texts about war. Make some judgements about the comparative strengths and weaknesses of the style and treatment of subject matter in the texts, and consider any other interpretations of the texts you are looking at.

Text 1

Isaac Rosenberg was a front-line soldier. This poem was written in 1916, two years before his death in action in the last year of the war.

BREAK OF DAY IN THE TRENCHES

The darkness crumbles away –
It is the same old druid Time as ever.
Only a live thing leaps my hand –
A queer sardonic rat –
As I pull the parapet's poppy
To stick behind my ear.
Droll rat, they would shoot you if they knew
Your cosmopolitan sympathies.
(And God knows what antipathies).
Now you have touched this English hand
You will do the same to a German –
Soon, no doubt, if it be your pleasure
To cross the sleeping green between.
It seems you inwardly grin as you pass
Strong eyes, fine limbs, haughty athletes
Less chanced than you for life,
Bonds to the whims of murder,
Sprawled in the bowels of the earth,
The torn fields of France.
What do you see in our eyes
At the shrieking iron and flame
Hurled through still heavens?
What quaver – what heart aghast?
Poppies whose roots are in man's veins
Drop, and are ever dropping;
But mine in my ear is safe,
Just a little white with the dust.

Text 2

This is an excerpt from *The Ghost Road*, the final part of *The Regeneration Trilogy* by Pat Barker. W. H. R. Rivers was an army psychologist who met Siegfried Sassoon at Craiglockhart hospital in 1917.

After Wansbeck had gone, Rivers sat quietly for a few minutes before adding a note to the file. Sassoon had been much in his mind while he was speaking to Wansbeck, Sassoon and the apparitions that gathered round his bed and demanded to know why he was not in France. Also, another of his patients at Craiglockhart, Harrington, who'd had dreadful nightmares, even by Craiglockhart standards, and the nightmares had continued into the semi-waking state, so that they acquired the character of hypnagogic hallucinations. He saw the severed head, torso and limbs of a dismembered body hurtling towards him out of the darkness. A variant of this was a face bending over him, the lips, nose and eyelids eaten away as if by leprosy. The face, in so far as it was identifiable at all, was the face of a close friend whom Harrington had seen blown to pieces. From these dreams he woke either vomiting or with a wet bed, or both.

At the time he witnessed his friend's death Harrington had already been suffering from headaches, split vision, nausea, vomiting, disorder of micturition, spells of forgetfulness and a persistent gross tremor of the hands, dating from an explosion two months before in which he'd been buried alive. Despite these symptoms he had remained on duty (shoot the MO, thought Rivers) until his friend's death precipitated a total collapse.

What was interesting about Harrington was that instead of treatment bringing about an elaboration of the nightmares, so that the horrors began to assume a more symbolic, less directly representational form – the normal path to recovery – something rather more remarkable had happened. His friend's body had begun to reassemble itself. Night after night the eaten-away features had fleshed out again. And Harrington talked to him. Long conversations, apparently, or they seemed long to him on waking, telling his friend about Rivers, about life at Craiglockhart, about the treatment he was receiving . . .

After several weeks of this, he awoke one day with his memory of the first hour after the explosion restored. He had, even in his traumatized state and under heavy fire, crawled round the pieces of his friend's body collecting items of equipment – belt, revolver, cap and lapel badges – to send to the mother. The knowledge that, far from having fled from the scene, he had behaved with exemplary courage and loyalty, did a great deal to restore Harrington's self-esteem, for, like most of the patients at Craiglockhart, he suffered from a deep sense of shame and failure. From then on the improvement was dramatic, though still the conversations with the dead friend continued, until one morning he awoke crying, and realized he was crying, not only for his own loss but also for his friend's, for the unlived years.

Text 3

Edgell Rickword fought on the Western Front and published many poems in periodicals. Most of them were written in the 1920s.

WINTER WARFARE

Colonel Cold strode up the Line
    (Tabs of rime and spurs of ice).
Stiffened all where he did glare,
    Horses, men, and lice.

Visited a forward post,
   Left them burning, ear to foot;
Fingers stuck to biting steel,
   Toes to frozen boot.

Stalked on into No Man's Land,
   Turned the wire to fleecy wool,
Iron stakes to sugar sticks
   Snapping at a pull.

Those who watched with hoary eyes
   Saw two figures gleaming there;
Hauptman Kälte, Colonel Cold,
   Gaunt, in the grey air.

Stiffly, tinkling spurs they moved
   Glassy eyed, with glinting heel
Stabbing those who lingered there
   Torn by screaming steel.

Text 4

This is an extract from *Oh What A Lovely War!*, which was devised by Joan Littlewood's Theatre Workshop Group, and first performed in 1953. The play tells the story of the First World War by setting the action in an Edwardian pierrot show, using slides of war action and songs of its time. At the beginning of this extract, the Nurse and the Medical Officer are discussing the problem of disposing of the huge number of unburied bodies.

MEDICAL OFFICER	We'll have to start burning them soon, nurse.
NURSE	Yes, it's such an unpleasant duty, doctor. The men always try to get out of it.
MEDICAL OFFICER	Oh, well, it'll be good farming country after.
NURSE	If there are any of us left to see it.
FIRST SOLDIER	Still got my water on the knee, doc.
MEDICAL OFFICER	I'll fix you up with a number nine later.
FIRST SOLDIER	On my knee! – I said, sir!
SERGEANT	All right, you men. I want this trench clear in half an hour; get stuck in. Come on, jump to it!
	[*The men form up, as in a slit trench, digging.*]
BAND	'Oh It's A Lovely War' [*Very slow*]
HAIG	[*reading a letter*] From Snowball to Douglas. Water and mud are increasing and becoming horrible. The longer days when they come will be most welcome, especially to

the officers, who say the conditions are impairing their efficiency. The other ranks don't seem to mind so much.

FIRST SOLDIER   Look out – we're awash! Hey, give us a hand; he's going under.

SECOND SOLDIER   Cor – he's worse than old Fred.

THIRD SOLDIER   Here, whatever happened to old Fred?

SECOND SOLDIER   I dunno. Haven't seen him since his last cry for help.

FOURTH SOLDIER   That's right; he got sucked under.

THIRD SOLDIER   Oh no, he went sick.

FIFTH SOLDIER   No, he went under.

THIRD SOLDIER   He went sick.

SECOND SOLDIER   He got sucked under, mate.

THIRD SOLDIER   Well, I bet you a fag he went sick.

SECOND SOLDIER   Don't be daft. You can't go sick here. You've got to lose your lungs, your liver, your lights . . .

SERGEANT   Watch it!

[*The Nurse crossing in front stumbles.*]

FIRST SOLDIER   I think she's lost hers.

NURSE   Thank you.

MEDICAL OFFICER   Put that man on a charge, sergeant.

FIRST SOLDIER   On a raft.

HAIG   Everything points to a complete breakdown in enemy morale. Now is the time to hit him resolutely and firmly. I understand the Prime Minister has been asking questions about my strategy. I cannot believe a British Minister could be so ungentlemanly.

[*The soldiers go off.*]

NURSE   [*writing*] Thank you for the copy of *The Times*. I am glad that in spite of all it is still a victory; it does not seem so here. It is beyond belief, the butchery; the men look so appalling when they are brought in and so many die.

HAIG   September 17th. Glass still falling. A light breeze blows from the south. Weather unsettled.

NEWSPANEL: *Average life of a machine gunner under attack . . . four minutes*

Text 5

REPORTED MISSING

My thought shall never be that you are dead:
Who laughed so lately in this quiet place.
The dear and deep-eyed humour of that face
Held something ever living, in Death's stead.
Scornful I hear the flat things they have said
And all their piteous platitudes of pain.
I laugh! I laugh! – For you will come again –
This heart would never beat if you were dead.
The world's adrowse in twilight hushfulness,
There's purple lilac in your little room,
And somewhere out beyond the evening gloom
Small boys are culling summer watercress.
Of these familiar things I have no dread
Being so very sure you are not dead.

Anna Gordon Keown

Text 6

DRAFTS

Waking to darkness; early silence broken
By seagulls' cries, and something undefined
And far away. Through senses half-awoken,
A vague enquiry drifts into one's mind.
What's happening? Down the hill a movement quickens
And leaps to recognition round the turning –
Then one's heart wakes, and grasps the fact, and sickens –
'Are we down-hearted' . . . 'Keep the homefires burning'.
They go to God-knows-where, with songs of Blighty,
While I'm in bed, and ribbons in my nightie.

Sex, nothing more, constituent no greater
Than those which make an eyebrow's slant or fall,
In origin, sheer accident, which, later,
Decides the biggest differences of all.
And, through a war, involves the chance of death
Against a life of physical normality –
So dreadfully safe! O, damn the shibboleth
Of sex! God knows we've equal personality.
Why should men face the dark while women stay
To live and laugh and meet the sun each day.

They've gone. The drumming escort throbs the distance,
And down the hill the seagulls' cries are rife
And clamorous. But in their shrill persistence
I think they're telling me – 'We're all one Life'.
As much one life as when we flamed together,
As linked, as indivisible, as then;
When nothing's separate, does it matter whether
We live as women or we die as men?
Or swoop as seagulls! Everything is part
Of one supreme intent, the deathless heart.

Nora Bomford

Text 7

THE CENOTAPH

September 1919
Not yet will those measureless fields be green again
Where only yesterday the wild sweet blood of wonderful youth was shed;
There is a grave whose earth must hold too long, too deep a stain,
Though for ever over it we may speak as proudly as we may tread.
But here, where the watchers by lonely hearths from the thrust of an
    inward sword have more slowly bled,
We shall build the Cenotaph: Victory, winged, with Peace, winged too, at
    the column's head.
And over the stairway, at the foot – oh! here, leave desolate, passionate
    hands to spread
Violets, roses, and laurel, with the small, sweet, twinkling country things
Speaking so wistfully of other Springs,
From the little gardens of little places where son or sweetheart was born
    and bred.
In splendid sleep, with a thousand brothers
               To lovers – to mothers
               Here, too, lies he:
Under the purple, the green, the red,
It is all young life: it must break some women's hearts to see
Such a brave, gay coverlet to such a bed!
Only, when all is done and said,
God is not mocked and neither are the dead.
For this will stand in our Market-place –
               Who'll sell, who'll buy
               (Will you or I
Lie each to each with the better grace)?
While looking into every busy whore's and huckster's face
As they drive their bargains, is the Face
Of God: and some young, piteous, murdered face.

Charlotte Mew

Preparing for the examination

In a sense, the whole course is a preparation for this examination, as you have worked on all the Assessment Objectives which are tested here. Hopefully you will have read a range of First World War texts, and some pre-twentieth-century texts, and thought about them in the ways suggested in this book. Some practice in the type of questions you will have to answer is a good idea, and you will find two sets of materials and questions below. The first set of materials and questions has some suggested responses to give you an idea of what the examiners will be looking for.

In the examination room

The Module 6 examination is different from any other that you sit for this A Level course, as you are presented with *unseen* material. Although you know what the prescribed area of study is, it is unlikely that you will have read the texts which you have to write about in the exam – they will be new to you on the day.

There are some important things to remember as you start the examination.

- You will have *two* questions to answer in three hours. The paper will advise you how to divide your time between the two questions, and will also tell you that the time includes 'reading time'. It must also include *thinking time* if you are to do well. You haven't seen these texts before; remember how much time you've spent reading and re-reading texts for your other exams before you felt prepared.

- After the first reading of the first extract, one element of all your subsequent reading should be comparative – looking for links between this extract and the others, and between this extract and texts you have read in the course of your background reading. At the same time, your planning should not consist of trying to signal every bit of reading you've done. You should be selecting appropriately, and not dragging as much wide reading in as you can at the expense of writing about the extracts.

- As you read, make some notes and underline key words and phrases in the extracts. Then take some more time to draw a plan together, in the light of the question. Although you will be anxious to get on with writing, there are so many things to think about here that planning is necessary for you to create a clear and coherent response. This will not only ensure that you are able to address all the Assessment Objectives 2, 3, 4 and 5, and be rewarded for addressing them, but it will also enhance your performance in Assessment Objective 1, the ability to 'communicate clearly the knowledge, understanding and insight appropriate to literary study, using appropriate terminology and accurate and coherent written expression'. This Assessment Objective is tested on both questions.

- When you've formed a plan, start to write, making sure you choose the right words for the task. Don't be afraid of changing your mind about the extracts as you work; after all, you've never seen them before, so as you revisit them during the course of writing you may well find new things to comment on. Incorporate these new thoughts into your writing, rather than starting again.

- As you write, keep your mind on two key elements – the question and the Assessment Objectives. You should be sure that what you are writing is a direct response to the question you've been asked, and that you don't lose your focus on it. It might be very tempting to insert as much as you can about the texts you've read about the First World War – but you could easily drift away from the question and the extracts on the paper if you follow that course. You should only refer to elements of your wide reading which are relevant to the question and comparable to the extracts. There are no prizes for particularly long answers, either – it's quality that counts, not quantity.

The question paper will remind you about the Assessment Objectives targeted by each question, but you should be able to identify them yourself by reading the questions carefully, and recognising what you are being asked to do.

Below are two sample question papers. Outline responses are given for the first paper. You could attempt the question first, and then compare your responses with the outlines, or do this first if you need to. The second sample question paper is for you to attempt on your own.

Sample Paper 1

1 Reading

- Here is the selection of material taken from the <u>prescribed area for study</u>. You will be using this material to answer the questions in this examination.

- Alongside the three pieces (B, C and D) about the First World War (the prescribed area for study) you will find a piece of pre-twentieth-century writing. This also has <u>war</u> as its theme.

- Read all four pieces and their introduction very carefully and closely. Then read them again several times in the light of the specific questions set.

2 The questions, what they test, and how to manage your time

All questions test your ability to:

- *communicate clearly*

- *explore and comment on the relationships between texts*

- *show detailed understanding of the ways in which writers' choices of form, structure and language shape meanings.*

Question 1a

- You should plan to spend about 1 hour and 15 minutes on question 1a; this will include reading time.

  This question especially tests your ability to:

  explore and comment on relationships and comparisons between literary texts

  and

  articulate independent judgements, informed by different interpretations of literary texts by other readers.

Question 1b

- You should spend about 1 hour and 45 minutes on question 1b; this will include reading time.

  This question especially tests your ability to:

  explore and comment on relationships and comparisons between literary texts

  and

  evaluate the significance of cultural, historical and other contextual influences on literary texts and study.

3 Wider reading

The paper tests your wider reading on the subject of *War in Literature* with specific reference to literature of and about the *First World War*.

In your answers, you should take every opportunity to refer to this wider reading and to your knowledge of this specific area of study.

Extract A

Walt Whitman (1819–92) was an American writer who published a collection of poems about the American Civil War.

FROM THE WOUND-DRESSER

2

[. . .] Bearing the bandages, water and sponge,
Straight and swift to my wounded I go,
Where they lie on the ground after the battle brought in,
Where their priceless blood reddens the grass the ground,
Or to the rows of the hospital tent, or under the roof'd hospital,
To the long rows of cots up and down each side I return,
To each and all one after another I draw near, not one do I miss,
An attendant follows holding a tray, he carries a refuse pail,
Soon to be fill'd with clotted rags and blood, emptied, and fill'd again.

I onward go, I stop,
With hinged knees and steady hand to dress wounds,
I am firm with each, the pangs are sharp yet unavoidable,
One turns to me his appealing eyes – poor boy! I never knew you,
Yet I think I could not refuse this moment to die for you, if that would
     save you.

3

On, on I go, (open doors of time! open hospital doors!)
The crush'd head I dress, (poor crazed hand tear not the bandage away,)
The neck of the cavalry-man with the bullet through and through I
     examine,
Hard the breathing rattles, quite glazed already the eye, yet life struggles
     hard,
(Come sweet death! be persuaded O beautiful death!
In mercy come quickly.)

From the stump of the arm, the amputated hand,
I undo the clotted lint, remove the slough, wash off the matter and blood,
Back on his pillow the soldier bends with curv'd neck and side falling head,
His eyes are closed, his face is pale, he dares not look on the bloody stump,
And has not yet look'd on it.

I dress a wound in the side, deep, deep,
But a day or two more, for see the frame all wasted and sinking,
And the yellow-blue countenance see.

I dress the perforated shoulder, the foot with the bullet-wound,
Cleanse the one with a gnawing and putrid gangrene, so sickening, so
     offensive,
While the attendant stands behind aside me holding the tray and pail.

I am faithful, I do not give out,
The fractur'd thigh, the knee, the wound in the abdomen,
These and more I dress with impassive hand, (yet deep in my breast a fire,
    a burning flame.)

4

Thus in silence in dreams' projections,
Returning, resuming, I thread my way through the hospitals,
The hurt and wounded I pacify with soothing hand,
I sit by the restless all the dark night, some are so young,
Some suffer so much, I recall the experience sweet and sad,
(Many a soldier's loving arms about this neck have cross'd and rested,
Many a soldier's kiss dwells on these bearded lips.)

Extract B

This is an extract from *Oh What A Lovely War!*, which was devised by Joan Littlewood's Theatre Workshop Group, and first performed in 1953. The play tells the story of the First World War by setting the action in an Edwardian pierrot show, using slides of war action and songs of its time.

Voices offstage sing 'Gassed Last Night' as a sequence of slides appear on the screen.

Slide 22: Infantry advancing along the crest of a hill, silhouetted against a large white cloud.

Slide 23: Two German infantrymen running to escape an advancing cloud of poison gas.

Slide 24: A group of 'walking wounded' Tommies, some with bandaged eyes owing to being gassed.

Slide 25: Group of four German soldiers, carrying one of their gassed in a blanket.

Slide 26: Line-up, Indian file, of gassed Tommies, all with bandaged eyes, and one hand on the shoulder of the person immediately in front of them.

Slide 27: Another picture of 'walking wounded': two French Poilus, eyes bandaged, walking hand in hand, escorted by another Frenchman and a Tommy.

Slide 28: Photograph of a German infantryman diving for cover, beside a field gun, as a shell explodes nearby.

Slide 29: Three British infantrymen, full pack, standing in mud and slush, firing over the parapet of a trench.

Slide 30: Three Germans in a dugout, silhouetted against clouds of smoke caused by a plane bombing overhead.

Slide 31: Four Tommies sitting in dugouts, which are merely holes, waist deep in mud.

Slide 32: A dead German soldier, lying in a slit trench.

SONG: '*Gassed Last Night*'.

[22] Gassed last night and gassed the night before, [23]
Going to get gassed tonight if we never get gassed any more. [24]
When we're gassed we're sick as we can be,
'Cos phosgene [25] and mustard gas is much too much for me.
They're warning [26] us, they're warning us,
One [27] respirator for the four of us.
Thank your lucky stars that three of us can run,
So one of us can use it all alone. [29]
Bombed last night and bombed the night before,
Going to get bombed tonight if we never get bombed any more.
When we're bombed we're [29] scared as we can be.
God strafe the bombing planes from High Germany.

They're [30] over us, they're over us,
One shell hole for just the [31] four of us,
Thank your lucky stars there are no more of us,
'Cos [32] one of us could fill it all alone.

A group of five British soldiers enter and build a barricade.

SERGEANT	Get this barricade up, quickly. Keep your heads down.
LIEUTENANT	Have you got the trench consolidated, sergeant?
SERGEANT	All present and correct, sir.
LIEUTENANT	The C.O. is going to have a word with the men.
SERGEANT	Right, lads – attention!
	[*The Commanding Officer enters.*]
COMMANDING OFFICER	You can stand the men at ease, sergeant.
	[*Sound of machine-gun fire. They throw themselves down.*]
LIEUTENANT	On your feet, lads.
SERGEANT	Come on – jump to it!
COMMANDING OFFICER	You can let them smoke if they want to.
SERGEANT	The C.O. says you can smoke. But don't let me catch you.
COMMANDING OFFICER	Now, you men, I've just come from having a powwow with the colonel; we think you've done some damn fine work – we congratulate you.

SOLDIERS	Thank you, sir.
COMMANDING OFFICER	I know you've had it pretty hard the last few days, bombs, shells, and snipers; we haven't escaped scot-free back at staff either, I can tell you. Anyway, we're all here – well, not all of us, of course; and that gas of ours was pretty nasty – damned wind changing.
LIEUTENANT	Indeed, sir.
COMMANDING OFFICER	But these mishaps do happen in war, and gas can be a war-winning weapon. Anyway, so long as we can all keep smiling; you're white men all. [*To the Lieutenant*] Sector all tidy now, Lieutenant?
LIEUTENANT	Well, we've buried most of the second Yorks and Lancs, sir; there's a few D.L.I.s and the men from our own company left.
COMMANDING OFFICER	I see. Well, look, let the lads drum up some char . . .
	[*Sound of exploding shell.*]
LIEUTENANT	Get down, sir.
COMMANDING OFFICER	Good God!
VOICE	[*offstage*] Stretcher bearers! . . . Stretcher bearers! . . .
COMMANDING OFFICER	You have no stretcher bearers over there?
LIEUTENANT	No, I'm afraid they went in the last attack, sir. I'm waiting for reliefs from H.Q.
COMMANDING OFFICER	Oh well, they're stout chaps!
	[*Explosion.*]
COMMANDING OFFICER	Yes, you'd better let the men keep under cover.
LIEUTENANT	Thank you, sir.
COMMANDING OFFICER	Damn place still reeks of decomposing bodies.
LIEUTENANT	I'm afraid it's unavoidable, sir; the trench was mainly full of Jerries.
COMMANDING OFFICER	Yes, of course, you were more or less sharing the same front line for a couple of days, weren't you?
LIEUTENANT	Yes, sir.
COMMANDING OFFICER	Oh well, carry on.
LIEUTENANT	Thank you, sir.
COMMANDING OFFICER	Ye Gods! What's that?
LIEUTENANT	Oh, it's a Jerry, sir.

COMMANDING OFFICER	What?
LIEUTENANT	It's a leg, sir.
COMMANDING OFFICER	Well, get rid of it, man. You can't have an obstruction sticking out of the parapet like that. [*He goes off.*]
LIEUTENANT	Hardcastle. Remove the offending limb.
SERGEANT	Well, we can't do that, sir; it's holding up the parapet. We've just consolidated the position.
LIEUTENANT	Well, get a shovel and hack it off; and then dismiss the men. [*He goes off.*]
SERGEANT	Right, sir. What the bloody hell am I going to hang my equipment on now. All right, lads, get back, get yourselves some char. Heads, trunks, blood all over the place, and all he's worried about is a damned leg. [*The soldiers go off.*]

Extract C

Below are extracts from two letters Robert Graves sent home in May 1915. They feature in his autobiography, *Goodbye To All That*.

May 28th. [. . .] Last night a lot of German stuff was flying about, including shrapnel. I heard one shell whish-whishing towards me and dropped flat. It burst just over the trench where 'Petticoat Lane' runs into 'Lowndes Square'. My ears sang as though there were gnats in them, and a bright scarlet light shone over everything. My shoulder got twisted in falling and I thought I had been hit, but I hadn't been. The vibration made my chest sing, too, in a curious way, and I lost my sense of equilibrium. I was ashamed when the sergeant-major came along the trench and found me on all fours, still unable to stand up straight.

A corpse is lying on the fire-step waiting to be taken down to the grave-yard tonight: a sanitary-man, killed last night in the open while burying lavatory stuff between our front and support lines. His arm was stretched out stiff when they carried him in and laid him on the fire-step; it stretched right across the trench. His comrades joke as they push it out of the way to get by. 'Out of the light, you old bastard! Do you own this bloody trench?' Or else they shake hands with him familiarly. 'Put it there, Billy Boy.' Of course, they're miners, and accustomed to death. They have a very limited morality, but they keep to it. It's moral, for instance, to rob anyone of anything, except a man in their own platoon. They treat every stranger as an enemy until he proves himself their friend, and then there's nothing they won't do for him. They are lecherous, the young ones at least, but without the false shame of the English lecher. I had a letter to censor the other day, written by a lance-corporal to his wife. He said that the French girls were nice to sleep with, so she mustn't worry on his account, but that he far preferred sleeping with her and missed her a great deal.

June 9th. I am beginning to realize how lucky I was in my gentle introduction to the Cambrin trenches. We are now in a nasty salient, a little to the south of the brick-stacks, where casualties are always heavy. The company had seventeen casualties yesterday from bombs and grenades. The front trench averages thirty yards from the Germans. Today, at one part, which is only twenty yards away from an occupied German sap, I went along whistling 'The Farmer's Boy' to keep up my spirits, when suddenly I saw a group bending over a man lying at the bottom of the trench. He was making a snoring noise mixed with animal groans. At my feet lay the cap he had worn, splashed with his brains. I had never seen human brains before; I somehow regarded them as a poetical figment. One can joke with a badly-wounded man and congratulate him on being out of it. One can disregard a dead man. But even a miner can't make a joke that sounds like a joke over a man who takes three hours to die, after the top part of his head has been taken off by a bullet fired at twenty yards' range.

Beaumont, of whom I told you in my last letter, also got killed – the last unwounded survivor of the original battalion, except for the transport men. He had his legs blown against his back. Everyone was swearing angrily, but an R.E. officer came up and told me that he had a tunnel driven under the German front line, and that if my chaps wanted to do a bit of bombing, now was the time. So he sent the mine up – it was not a big one, he said, but it made a tremendous noise and covered us with dirt – and we waited for a few seconds for the other Germans to rush up to help the wounded away, and then chucked all the bombs we had.

Beaumont had been telling how he had won about five pounds' worth of francs in the sweepstake after the Rue du Bois show: a sweepstake of the sort that leaves no bitterness behind it. Before a show, the platoon pools all its available cash and the survivors divide it up afterwards. Those who are killed can't complain, the wounded would have given far more than that to escape as they have, and the unwounded regard the money as a consolation prize for still being here.

Extract D

AN INCIDENT

He was just a boy, as I could see,
For he sat in the tent there close by me.
I held the lamp with its flickering light,
And felt the hot tears blur my sight
As the doctor took the blood-stained bands
From both his brave, shell-shattered hands –
His boy hands, wounded more pitifully
Than Thine, O Christ, on Calvary.

I was making tea in the tent where they,
The wounded, came in their agony;
And the boy turned when his wounds were dressed,
Held up his face like a child at the breast,
Turned and held his tired face up,
For he could not hold the spoon or cup,
And I fed him. . . . Mary, Mother of God,
All women tread where thy feet have trod.

And still on the battlefield of pain
Christ is stretched on His Cross again;
And the Son of God in agony hangs,
Womanhood striving to ease His pangs.
For each son of man is a son divine,
Not just to the mother who calls him 'mine',
As he stretches out his stricken hand,
Wounded to death for the Mother Land.

Mary H. J. Henderson

Answer **all** questions.

1a Basing your answer on Extract A and <u>one</u> of the other three extracts, write a comparison of the ways the writers present attitudes to injury and death in war.

How far do you agree with the view that Whitman presents his subject in a far more sentimental and unrealistic way than the writer of the extract of your choice?

1b By comparing **Extracts B, C and D,** and by referring to your own wider reading, examine how typical in both style and treatment of subject matter these writings are of literature from or about the First World War.

You should consider:

• language, form and structure

- the ways the writers use the genre of their choice to express their thoughts and feelings

- the writers' attitudes to war and contemporary society

- the influence of the time of composition

- the gender of the writers.

Deconstructing the questions

Question 1a

- 'Write a comparison' invites you to *'explore and comment on the relationships and comparisons between literary texts'* (AO2ii).

- 'the ways the writers present' invites you to *'show detailed understanding of the ways in which writers' choices of form, structure and language shape meanings'* (AO3), as does 'presents his subject' in the second part of the question.

- 'How far do you agree with' invites you to *'articulate independent opinions and judgements, informed by different interpretations of literary texts by other readers'* (AO4).

- Another key element here is choice. You have to choose which extract to compare with **A**, bearing the question in mind, which here concerns 'attitudes to injury and death in war'. So, which extract seems most easily comparable with **A**? Which extract can you most easily analyse in terms of presentation? Which extract offers you the chance to refer to some of your wider reading? Don't try and do a lot of analysis on each extract to make this choice, though – make a choice and then start to work.

Question 1b

- 'By comparing' asks you again to *'explore and comment on the relationships and comparisons between literary texts'* (AO2ii).

- 'referring to your own wider reading' is a specific invitation to refer to other texts, so this is a more important element here than it is in **1a**, perhaps, addressing 'how typical'.

- 'style and treatment of subject matter' asks you to *'show detailed understanding of the ways in which writers' choices of form, structure and language shape meanings'* (AO3). The first two elements 'language, form and structure' and 'the ways the writers use the genre of their choice to express their thoughts and feelings' also address AO3.

- 'how typical' and the list of elements tests your ability to *'evaluate the significance of cultural, historical and other contextual influences on literary texts and study'* (AO5ii).

Example of response to 1a

Here are some notes which could be shaped into a response to **1a**, assuming that **Extract B** was chosen as the extract for comparison. At the end of this there are some notes on aspects of the other two extracts which might be used in a comparison with **A**.

Extract B

First part of question.

- Suffering of soldiers (injury or death) are presented differently – **A** in first person verse, **B** in song, slides, dialogue, giving multiple viewpoints.

- Slides in **B** show British, German, French – emphasise suffering of all sides – only one side in **A**. Implies universal attitude of writer. Perhaps refer to Owen 'Strange Meeting', end of *Birdsong* extract in Module 5 material, others showing both sides.

- Focus of **A** always on emotions of narrator, through to end. **B** more diverse, though slides/song in combination give an unrelenting focus on suffering and death, either potentially or actually.

- Both writers use repetition to shape and convey their attitudes. Sense of rush and purpose in **A** given by repetition of 'on, on', working throughout with unconventional use of commas where full stops should be – a sense of a continuous, never-ending task. 'Deep, deep' for emotive effect. In **B**, song form naturally uses repetitions, here picking out key words – 'gassed' 5 times in first verse, 'Bombed' in second. 'Last night/the night before', 'much too much for me', and 'they're warning us, they're warning us' all repetitions implying attitude. Refer to other songs if known.

- Both extracts use graphic words and images – 'matter and blood', 'the bloody stump', 'gnawing and putrid gangrene' (**A**), 'damn place still reeks of decomposing bodies' (**B**). Refer quickly to a similar example in wider reading. Presentation of attitudes different, though – direct giving of feelings in **A** 'so sickening, so offensive', which combines with direct appeal to an imagined onlooker: 'For see the frame all wasted . . . the yellow-blue countenance see'.

- Attitude of writer indirectly given in **B**, reflecting genre. Difference between officers and men in **B** – form of **A** doesn't allow this. Understatement of officer in 'pretty nasty', unrealistic encouragement of 'so long as we can all keep smiling'. Callousness of officers implied in 'all tidy', meaning how many bodies buried, and in refs to leg – 'an obstruction', 'get a shovel and hack it off'. None of this in **A**.

- Humour in **B** too, unlike seriousness of **A**. Black humour – 'well, not all of us, of course', 'What the bloody hell am I going to hang my equipment on now?' (could refer to Grave's remark about brains on cap in **Extract C** – 'even a miner can't make a joke . . .').

Second part of question – **A** more sentimental and unrealistic?

- Yes, with this pairing. (*Remember this is only an example – you have to say and support what you think, taking other interpretations into account.*)

- **A** uses sentiment directly 'priceless blood', 'appealing eyes', 'poor boy', 'poor crazed hand', and so on. Sentimental about death, too; 'sweet death', 'O beautiful death!' Injured soldier's attitude described 'with curv'd neck and side falling head', like a Rossetti portrait. The experience is 'sweet and sad'. Most sentiment reserved for narrator himself – seems to be the hero of his own story: 'I am faithful, I do not give out', 'not one do I miss', 'I am firm', and the romantic idea of the soldier's 'appealing eyes' causing the doctor to offer his own life to save him. Easy reference to Brooke's 'The Soldier' here. Does not ignore some of the 'realistic' graphic detail, however.

- **B** not sentimental, despite use of popular song. Uses understatement rather than exaggeration of **A** – 'tidy' could be seen as this instead of callous. Lieutenant makes bald statements without adjectives, saying 'we've buried most of the second Yorks and Lancs'. The Sergeant's reply is practical and realistic, but also chilling. Could refer to Owen's 'Insensibility'. Could lead to a view of **A** as being more acceptable to modern reader as there is sentiment expressed. We *should* feel something about this awful suffering.

Extract C

If you had chosen to compare **A** with **C**, here are some of the things you might have thought about:

- The direct attitude of the narrator/writer to the fear of injury and death is similar to the narrator of **A**, at least in the direct 'telling' of feeling; the narrator in **C** is self-critical, though, unlike **A**: 'I was ashamed . . .'. The writer of **C** feels he 'can joke with a badly-wounded man'; **A** has no room for this, who doesn't 'struggle' to 'disregard a dead man', though he does note with approval his own 'impassive hand'.

- There is clearly humour in the attitude of the soldiers to the dead man's arm, 'Put it there, Billy Boy', but the writer forgives the men for any apparent callousness – 'they're miners, and accustomed to death'. In this way the writer uses their attitude to stress the horror of what he sees – more subtle than approach of the narrator in **A**, despite this being autobiographical.

- Both writers use graphic details for effect, the 'blood and matter' of **A**, and the cap 'splashed with his brains' in **C**. Compare other similar texts, e.g. Owen's 'Dulce Et Decorum Est'.

- Clearly the attitudes of the soldiers to death are very unsentimental – the sweepstake story in the last para. of the June 9th letter. Nothing of the sort of adjectives that are used in **A**.

- Realism partly result of genre – this is autobiographical non-fiction, and told without much direct authorial comment, even in a letter, where more personal comment might be expected. Compare with other letters in wider reading.

Extract D

If you had chosen to compare **A** with **D**, here are some of the things you might have thought about:

- As in **A**, first-person poem centring on care of wounded. However, no sense of this narrator's views about her own actions, unlike **A**. **A** very personal – many instances of 'I' – **D** much less so, and depersonalises and deglorifies her own actions by universalising them, through reference to Mother of God: 'All women tread where thy feet have trod'. This could be aggrandisement, comparing herself to Mary, but not with '*all* women'.

- **D** also refers to 'just a boy', and shows a strong emotional effect – 'felt the hot tears blur my sight'. **A** mentions 'a fire, a burning flame' but 'deep in my breast' rather than openly manifested. This may reflect character, or gender. **D** refers to the boy as 'like a child at the breast' – again perhaps reflecting the gender of the writer, though the pose seems more natural and less artistic than the attitude of the soldier described in **A**. This again reflects the attitude of the speaker.

- **D** seems more deliberately wrought than **A** – uses structure and language to emphasise the religious nature of the feelings. **A** is an unbroken narrative stream, but **D** becomes completely universal in stanza 3 to express the writer's attitude to injury and death, 'each son of man is a son divine', likening each soldier's death to Christ on the cross, and the mother becoming 'the Mother Land', a patriotic concept not touched on in **A**.

For the second part of the question.

- **D** seems comparatively more sentimental than either **B** or **C** when compared with **A**. 'The lamp with its flickering light', the tears, the 'blood-stained' bands, the 'brave' hands, conjure a scene and an attitude more directly comparable in sentiment with **A**, and lacking even that poem's graphic detail. A final view, though, might depend on your response to the strong religious agenda here, as to whether you consider the poem 'sentimental' or 'unrealistic'. With reference 'unrealistic', **A** does stay with the incident described, whereas **D** moves beyond it into more abstract realms – more 'unrealistic', then?

Example of response to 1b

There are a number of ways of organising your response, once you've read through the extracts carefully, noting elements of the individual pieces and how they might relate to each other and to texts you have covered in your wider reading. You could follow the list of prompts in the question, choose one extract as key and compare the other two to it, or find another method. Below are some of the relevant things you might have found in each of the extracts, with comparative links to other extracts and wider reading. The organisation is up to you.

Extract B

- Form of songs, slides in drama unusual – no equivalent in lit. about period.

- Structure episodic – free-wheeling style typical of later period – time of writing significant influence.

- Song typical of songs of time, though – compare to any known. Heavy rhythm picks out 'gassed', 'bombed', etc.

- Expression of thoughts/feelings/attitudes to audience indirect – they have to infer them from slides/songs, dialogue. No authorial voice, unlike other two extracts.

- Words of song insist on camaraderie ('we', 'us', not 'I') – as in much lit., such as **C**, and other texts known (refer). 1 in 4 significant – it was the basic unit of men in the front line, referred to in accounts. Fallen soldiers had to be replaced in the 4.

- Bad conditions in trenches stressed here, as in much other war lit. – gas, waist-deep mud, shell-holes, numbers of dead in trench, military blunders – compare last line of Sassoon 'The General' – 'but he did for them both by his plan of attack' and many other refs to all elements. Gas refs here almost light-hearted – contrast with Owen's 'Dulce Et Decorum Est'.

- Leg in trench episode also referred to in **C**, and famous war photo. Attitudes here and in Graves comparable.

- Ref. to 'sharing the same trench' indication of static nature of war and close proximity. Also suggests that experiences of Allies and Germans were similar – compare Owen's 'Strange Meeting', Faulks's *Birdsong*, Graves's poem 'A Dead Boche', Sassoon's 'Reconciliation'.

- Stratified military system here reflects class system of the time. Ordinary soldiers not involved in this discussion. CO not used to front line – surprised by shell, explosion – compare Sassoon 'Base Details'. Understatement in language – compare **C** 'a lot of German stuff flying about'.

Extract C

- This extract is non-fiction – autobiography and letters within it. Compare similar forms in accounts, *Letters from a Lost Generation*, *Testament of Youth*, etc.

- Onomatopoeia of 'whish-whishing' compares with Owen's 'Anthem for Doomed Youth' and 'The Last Laugh'. Sensations of the individual in battle personal/direct, unlike **B**, **D** – sound, sight, and shame.

- Narrower canvas than **D** – reflects genre, and letter form. Letter is immediate – no wider perspective, or hindsight, possible.

- Trench conditions, as in **B**, at centre of extract. Corpse and arm a direct reminder of **B** and photo of arm in trench wall. Grim humour here, but in next letter humour is impossible, indicating depth of effect of brains on cap. Even miners 'accustomed to death' moved – further indication. Insensibility to death – compare Owen's 'Insensibility' – also shown in account of sweepstake. Morality of troops also here, not in other extracts.

- Brothels behind lines – ref. to other lit. Mining in front line in Owen's 'Strange Meeting', Faulks's *Birdsong*.

- Camaraderie and fierce loyalty to members of same platoon also in **B**. Letter June 1915 mentions 'last survivor of original battalion' – death rate in trenches – historical stats.

- Voice of officer in letters – shows in language, maybe attitude, but less sharply distinguished than in **B** – maybe reflecting less exaggeration in factual text, maybe viewpoint or character of narrator.

Extract D

- Content and diction more emotional than **B**, **C** – mentions of bravery and pain. 'agony', 'tears' might be expected in situation, but only mentioned here in three of the extracts.

- Focus here not trench conditions, but result – 'shell-shattered hands', though wounded and bandaged soldiers feature in slides in **B**. Religious attitudes and questioning of religion widespread in lit. – ref. to some. Owen 'At a Calvary near the Ancre': 'One ever hangs where shelled roads part' – though 'love of God seems dying' ('Exposure').

- No elements of humour here – passionate. Patriotism of 'Mother Land' might remind of Brooke's 'The Soldier', but no sense of glory/richness here.

- Gender central to this text – ref. to contemporary society in issue of women's occupations and position in society, and coming change.

- Focus on woman child – language refers to 'like a child at the breast'. Speaker identifies with 'Mary, Mother of God'.

- Stanza 3 conceptualises, universalises war experience, unlike **B** or **C**. Prepared for by move at end of stanza 2. Soldier likened to Christ 'each son of man is a son divine', and each soldier's mother to Mary, and to the 'Mother Land'.

Sample Paper 2

1 Reading

- Here is the selection of material taken from the <u>prescribed area for study</u>. You will be using this material to answer the questions in this examination.

- Alongside the three pieces (B, C and D) about the First World War (the prescribed area for study) you will find a piece of pre-twentieth-century writing. This also has <u>war</u> as its theme.

- Read all four pieces and their introduction very carefully and closely. Then read them again several times in the light of the specific questions set.

2 The questions, what they test, and how to manage your time

All questions test your ability to:

- *communicate clearly*

- *explore and comment on the relationships between texts*

- *show detailed understanding of the ways in which writers' choices of form, structure and language shape meanings.*

Question 1a

- You should plan to spend about 1 hour and 15 minutes on question 1a; this will include reading time.

  This question especially tests your ability to:

  explore and comment on relationships and comparisons between literary texts

  and

  articulate independent judgements, informed by different interpretations of literary texts by other readers.

Question 1b

- You should spend about 1 hour and 45 minutes on question 1b; this will include reading time.

  This question especially tests your ability to:

  explore and comment on relationships and comparisons between literary texts

  and

  evaluate the significance of cultural, historical and other contextual influences on literary texts and study.

3 Wider reading

The paper tests your wider reading on the subject of *War in Literature* with specific reference to literature of and about the *First World War*.

In your answers, you should take every opportunity to refer to this wider reading and to your knowledge of this specific area of study.

Extract A

FROM THE FRUITS OF WAR

I set aside to tell the restless toil,
The mangled corpse, the maimed limbs at last,
The shortened years by fret of fever's foil,
The smoothest skin with scabs and scars disgraced,
The frolic favour frounced and foul defaced,
The broken sleeps, the dreadful dreams, the woe,
Which wone with war and cannot from him go.
I list not write, for it becomes me not,
The secret wrath which God doth kindle oft,
To see the sucklings put into the pot,
To hear their guiltless blood send cries aloft,
And call for vengeance unto him, but soft!
The soldiers they commit those heinous acts,
Yet kings and captains answer for such facts.

What need we now at large for to rehearse
The force of Fortune, when she list to frown?
Why should I here display in barren verse
How realms are turned topsy-turvy down,
How kings and Caesars lost both claim and crown,
Whose haughty hearts to hent all honour haunt,
Till high mishaps their doughtiest deed do daunt?

All these, with more, my pen shall overpass,
Since Haughty Heart has fixed his fancy thus.
'Let chance,' saith he, 'be fickle as it was,
Sit bonus, in re mala, animus.
Nam omne solum viro forti ius.
And fie,' saith he, 'for goods or filthy gain!
I gape for glory; all the rest is vain.'

Vain is the rest, and that most vain of all:
A smouldering smoke which flieth with every wind,
A tickle treasure, like a trendling ball,
A passing pleasure mocking but the mind,
A fickle fee as fancy well can find,
A summer's fruit which long can never last,
But ripeneth soon and rots again as fast.

And tell me, Haughty Heart, confess a truth,
What man was aye so safe in glory's port
But trains of treason (oh, the more the ruth!)
Could undermine the bulwarks of this fort
And raze his ramparts down in sundry sort?
Search all thy books and thou shalt find therein
That honour is more hard to hold than win.

Ask Julius Caesar if this tale be true,
The man who conquered all the world so wide,
Whose only word commanded all the crew
Of Roman knights at many a time and tide,
Whose pomp was thought so great it could not glide –
At last with bodkins dubbed and doused to death,
And all his glory banished with his breath.

George Gascoigne (1525–77)

Extract B

Not About Heroes, by Stephen MacDonald is about the friendship between Wilfred Owen and Siegfried Sassoon, and their meeting at Craiglockhart hospital. In this extract from the play, Owen has left the hospital and returned to the front, where he was to die.

	[*Sound: the continuous rumbling of war noises. Owen moves to the dug-out position; stands there.*]
Sassoon	'He stood alone in some queer sunless place Where Armageddon ends. Perhaps he longed For days he might have lived, but his young face Gazed forth untroubled . . .'
Owen	I feel confident because I know I came out to help: directly, by leading them as well as an officer can; indirectly, by watching their sufferings so that I may plead for them as well as I can. I have done the first . . .
	[*Owen sits on the floor. Sassoon starts to take the blanket from his knees.* *Sound: noises fade down, under the speech.*]
Sassoon	[*folding the blanket*] The news from the Front was changing. We began to advance. The German troops had been told that this battle would decide the outcome of the war. They lost it – and with it, their faith in ultimate victory. At the end of September we began the Great Attack, and we passed the Hindenburg Line.
	[*Sound: an explosion – thunder, or a bomb, or gun. War noises continue.*]
Owen	Very dear Siegfried. I have been in action some days. Our experiences passed the limits of abhorrence: I lost all my earthly faculties and fought like an angel. You'll guess what happened when I say that I am now commanding the Company – and in the line I had a seraphic boy-lance-corporal as my sergeant-major.

I have mentioned my excellent batman, Jones. In the first wave of the attack he was shot in the head and thrown on top of me. He lay there, dead, his blood soaking my shoulder for half an hour. It's still there, crimson, on my tunic.

[*Sound: fades down as Sassoon speaks.*]

SASSOON

'I saw his round mouth's crimson deepen as it fell,
Like a Sun, in his last deep hour;
Watched the magnificent recession of farewell,
Clouding, half gleam, half glower,
And a last splendour burn the heavens of his cheek,
And in his eyes
The cold stars lighting, very old and bleak,
In different skies.'

[*Sound: an explosion. Noises continue.*]

OWEN

I can't say I suffered anything – having let my brain grow dull. My nerves, then, are in perfect order. My senses are charred. I shall feel again as soon as I dare, but now I must not. I don't take the cigarette out of my mouth when I write 'Deceased' across their letters . . .

Siegfried, I don't know what you'll think, but I've been recommended for the M.C. – and I've recommended every single N.C.O. who was with me. I'm glad of it – for the confidence it will give me at home.

[*Sound: an explosion. Noises continue. While Sassoon reads the official citation, Owen pins on the medal ribbon.*]

SASSOON

'For conspicuous gallantry and devotion to duty in the attack on the Fonsomme Line on 1st/2nd October 1918. On the Company Commander becoming a casualty, he assumed command and showed fine leadership and resisted a heavy counter-attack. He personally manipulated a captured enemy Machine Gun in an isolated position and inflicted considerable losses on the enemy. Throughout he behaved most gallantly.'

Extract C

Goodbye To All That is the autobiography of Robert Graves, in which he writes about his experiences as a young officer in the First World War.

We had spent the day after the attack carrying the dead down for burial and cleaning the trench up as best we could. That night the Middlesex held the line, while the Royal Welch carried all the unbroken gas-cylinders along to a position on the left flank of the brigade, where they were to be used on the following night, September 27th. This was worse than carrying the dead; the cylinders were cast-iron, heavy and hateful. The men cursed and sulked. Only the officers knew of the proposed attack; the men must not be told until just beforehand. I felt like screaming. Rain was still pouring down, harder than ever. We knew definitely, this time, that ours would be only a diversion to help troops on our right make the real attack.

The scheme was the same as before: at 4 p.m. gas would be discharged for forty minutes, and after a quarter of an hour's bombardment we should attack. I broke the news to the men about three o'clock. They took it well. The relations of officers and men, and of senior and junior officers, had been very different in the excitement of battle. There had been no insubordination, but a greater freedom of speech, as though we were all drunk together. I found myself calling the adjutant 'Charley' on one occasion; he appeared not to mind in the least. For the next ten days my relations with my men were like those I had in the Welsh Regiment; later, discipline reasserted itself, and it was only occasionally that I found them intimate.

At 4 p.m. then, the gas went off again with a strong wind; the gas-men had brought enough spanners this time. The Germans stayed absolutely silent. Flares went up from the reserve lines, and it looked as though all the men in the front trench were dead. The brigadier decided not to take too much for granted; after the bombardment he sent out a Cameronian officer and twenty-five men as a feeling-patrol. The patrol reached the German wire; there came a burst of machine-gun and rifle fire, and only two wounded men regained the trench.

We waited on the fire-step from four to nine o'clock, with fixed bayonets, for the order to go over. My mind was a blank, except for the recurrence of *S'nice S'mince S'pie, S'nice S'mince S'pie . . . I don't like ham, lamb or jam, and I don't like roley-poley . . .*

The men laughed at my singing. The acting C.S.M. said: 'It's murder, sir.'

'Of course it's murder, you bloody fool,' I agreed. 'But there's nothing else for it, is there?' It was still raining. *But when I sees a s'nice s'mince s'pie, I asks for a helping twice . . .*

At nine o'clock brigade called off the attack; we were told to hold ourselves in readiness to go over at dawn.

No order came at dawn, and no more attacks were promised us after this. From the morning of September 24th to the night of October 3rd, I had in all eight hours of sleep. I kept myself awake and alive by drinking about a bottle of whisky a day. I had never drunk it before, and have seldom drunk it since; it certainly helped me then. We had no blankets, greatcoats, or waterproof sheets, nor any time or material to build new shelters. The rain poured down. Every night we went out to fetch in the dead of the other battalions. The Germans continued indulgent and we had few casualties. After the first day or two the corpses swelled and stank. I vomited more than once while superintending the carrying. Those we could not get in from the German wire continued to swell until the wall of the stomach collapsed, either naturally or when punctured by a bullet; a disgusting smell would float across. The colour of the dead faces changed from white to yellow-grey, to red, to purple, to green, to black, to slimy.

On the morning of the 27th a cry arose from No Man's Land. A wounded soldier of the Middlesex had recovered consciousness after two days. He lay close to the German wire. Our men heard it and looked at each other. We had a tender-hearted lance-corporal named Baxter. He was the man to boil up a special dixie for the sentries of his section when they came off duty. As soon as he heard the wounded Middlesex man, he ran along the trench calling for a volunteer to help fetch him in. Of course, no one would go; it was death to put one's head over the parapet. When he came running to ask me I excused myself as being the only officer in the company. I would come out with him at dusk, I said – not now. So he went alone. He jumped quickly over the parapet, then strolled across No Man's Land, waving a handkerchief; the Germans fired to frighten him, but since he persisted they let him come up close. Baxter continued towards them and, when he got to the Middlesex man, stopped and pointed to show the Germans what he was at. Then he dressed the man's wounds, gave him a drink of rum and some biscuit that he had with him, and promised to be back again at nightfall. He did come back, with a stretcher-party, and the man eventually recovered. I recommended Baxter for the Victoria Cross, being the only officer who had witnessed the action, but the authorities thought it worth no more than a Distinguished Conduct Medal.

The Actor and I had decided to get in touch with the battalion on our right. It was the Tenth Highland Light Infantry. I went down their trench some time in the morning of the 26th and walked nearly a quarter of a mile without seeing a sentry or an officer. There were dead men, sleeping men, wounded men, gassed men, all lying anyhow. The trench had been used as a latrine. Finally I met a Royal Engineer officer who said: 'If the Boche knew what an easy job he had, he'd just walk over and take this trench.'

Extract D

Siegfried Sassoon served as an officer in the First World War. This poem was written in hospital, ten days after he was wounded in action.

THE REAR-GUARD

(HINDENBURG LINE, APRIL 1917)

Groping along the tunnel, step by step,
He winked his prying torch with patching glare
From side to side, and sniffed the unwholesome air.

Tins, boxes, bottles, shapes too vague to know;
A mirror smashed, the mattress from a bed;
And he, exploring fifty feet below
The rosy gloom of battle overhead.

Tripping, he grabbed the wall; saw some one lie
Humped at his feet, half-hidden by a rug,
And stooped to give the sleeper's arm a tug.
'I'm looking for headquarters.' No reply.
'God blast your neck!' (For days he'd had no sleep)
'Get up and guide me through this stinking place.'

Savage, he kicked a soft, unanswering heap,
And flashed his beam across the livid face
Terribly glaring up, whose eyes yet wore
Agony dying hard ten days before;
And fists of fingers clutched a blackening wound.

Alone he staggered on until he found
Dawn's ghost that filtered down a shafted stair
To the dazed, muttering creatures underground
Who hear the boom of shells in muffled sound.
At last, with sweat of horror in his hair,
He climbed through darkness to the twilight air,
Unloading hell behind him step by step.

22 April 1917

Answer **all** questions.

1a Basing your answer on Extract A and *either* **Extract B** or **Extract C**, write a comparison of the ways the writers present glory and heroism in war.

How far do you agree with the view that Gascoigne is more interested in 'kings and captains' than the harsh realities of war?

1b By comparing **Extracts B, C and D**, and by referring to your own wider reading, examine how typical in both style and treatment of subject matter these writings are of literature from or about the First World War.

You should consider:

- language, form and structure
- the ways the writers use the genre of their choice to express their thoughts and feelings
- the writers' attitudes to war and the feelings of characters about war
- the influence of the time of composition.

Achieving top marks in the mark schemes

Assessment Objectives 1, 2 and 3 are tested in both **1a** and **1b**. These are the descriptors for achievement in these Assessment Objectives in Band 4, 16–20 marks out of 20:

- analysis of texts in detail
- extended and illuminating comparison
- technically accurate
- telling and accurate use of appropriate critical vocabulary
- sophisticated analysis of ways in which form, structure and language shape meanings.

In addition, **1a** tests AO4. The Band 4 descriptors are:

- cogent, well-structured argument
- mature and confident judgement based on informed consideration of various possibilities.

1b tests AO5ii. The Band 4 descriptors are:

- specific detailed and illuminating connections between texts and context
- understanding of texts in tradition
- analysis of importance of contextual factors in writing.

Glossary

Archetype the prototype or original model.

Aves a reference in Keats's poem 'The Eve of St Agnes' to the prayers said by the Beadsman to the Virgin Mary, 'Hail Mary, full of Grace . . .'.

Bacchus the Greek god of wine.

Beadsman a pensioner who had to pray to his own saintly religious figure.

Caricature a grotesque presentation of a person or thing which relies on over-exaggeration of one particular trait.

Demotic popular, colloquial or vulgar language.

Diabolical words, thoughts or actions connected in some way to the devil.

Dialect a form of language related to a particular place, class or person which has distinctive forms of speech and expression.

Didactic in literature, that which has the intention to instruct.

Divine Right the belief that God, independent of subjects' wills, selected the ruler.

Fall from Paradise mankind's fall from the Garden of Eden when Adam ate the forbidden fruit.

Fusion blending of different things into one, as in Wordsworth's poem *The Prelude*.

Half-rhyme a type of versification when the rhyme is not full, for example, rhyme created by assonance.

Heroic rhyming couplets iambic pentameters rhyming in pairs, originally used by Pope and Dryden, but also used by writers such as Chaucer and Keats.

Incantatory language which sounds as though it is the recitation of a spell or a charm.

Legalism a preference for the law itself rather than the principles of the Bible and Christian virtue, as in *The Merchant of Venice*.

Medieval/medievalism in nineteenth-century poetry, the practice of imitating the Middle Ages.

Milieu the particular environment, social, academic, literary, etc. in which a writer lives.

Morality plays medieval dramas in verse in which abstractions such as Vice and Virtue were presented on stage, for example, *Everyman*.

Motif a dominant idea or image which reappears throughout a work, such as the use of financial images in *Women Beware Women*.

Narrative poem a poem in which a story is told.

Natural universe all existing things which relate to nature. This may be a contrast to the divine universe, in which all of creation is related to God.

Negative capability a term used to interpret Keats's idea of experience. A belief that one can accept experience without the need for proof or reason; of being able, therefore, to live in a state of uncertainty.

Orthodox the holding of 'correct' or generally accepted opinions, especially related to religion.

Pantheism a doctrine which holds that God may be perceived in all things, and that all things are divine.

Paradox a self-contradictory statement or series of statements.

Pastoral poems which portray country life.

Register a set of words used in specific circumstances or time period.

Satire literary work in which the aim is to amuse, criticise or correct by means of ridicule, for example, Jonson's *Volpone*.

Sensual related to the senses or sensations, usually with a sexual connotation rather than spiritual or intellectual.

Sensuous appealing to the senses, not restricted to fleshy or sexual pleasure.

Seven deadly sins in theology, the seven sins for which, if unrepented, mankind will go to Hell. They are: Pride, Covetousness, Lust, Gluttony, Anger, Envy and Sloth.

Social hierarchy the different ranks of people within society.

Socialist a person who approves of the state ownership, of the means of production and distribution, and financial exchanges of goods and money.

Soliloquise to speak alone or to oneself. Used as a theatrical device in plays for characters to give speeches without the presence of others on the stage.

Sublime having a quality of grandeur which inspires awe, as Wordsworth perceives in nature.

Syntax the grammatical arrangement of words in a sentence or in speech.

Vice figure the character(s) representing evil, originally on the medieval stage.

Visionary a person given to seeing visions or holding fanciful theories; things which exist only in the imagination.